T0266177

SECRETS OF VOODOO

SECRETS
OF
VOODOO

Milo Rigaud

Translated from the French by
ROBERT B. CROSS

Photographs by
ODETTE MENNESSON-RIGAUD

CITY LIGHTS BOOKS
SAN FRANCISCO

First published in the United States of America by Arco Publishing, Inc. 1969
Published by City Lights Books 1985
Reprinted by arrangement with Arco Publishing, Inc., New York

Cover painting *Voodoo Dance* by Rosemarie Deruisseau

Library of Congress Cataloging-in-Publication Data

Rigaud, Milo, 1914-
     Secrets of Voodoo

       Reprint. Originally published: New York, N.Y.:
Arco, c 1969.
        1. Voodooism–Haiti. 2. Folklore–Haiti.
        3.Haiti–Religion. I. Title.
BL2490.R5313 1985   299' 67 85-19054
ISBN: 0-87286-171-6 /   978-0-87286-171-8

Visit our website: www.citylights.com

CITY LIGHTS BOOKS are edited by Lawrence Ferlinghetti and Nancy J. Peters
and published at the City Lights Bookstore, 261 Columbus Avenue,
San Francisco, CA 94133.

Contents

1

Origins and Elements of Voodoo

T O the uninitiated, Voodoo has long been thought of as a primitive form of magic and belief in ghosts. Most of what the average layman knows of Voodoo comes only from misleading use of it in Hollywood horror movies and in paperback thrillers that emphasize "witch doctors" or the sticking of pins in "Voodoo dolls."

But the fact is that Voodoo encompasses an exceedingly complex religion and magic with complicated rituals and symbols that have developed for thousands of years—perhaps longer than any other of today's established faiths. The believer in Voodoo—and there are millions of blacks and some whites who practice it—centers his hopes and fears as strongly on it as does a follower of Christianity, Judaism, Buddhism, or Islam. Indeed, the Haitian atmosphere seems ever impregnated with it—as if with a rich, mystical aroma of Africa—to the extent that individuals as well as families are conscious of Voodoo's effect upon their lives with a curious mixture of glory and dread.

This book—the result of more than thirty years of study—will endeavor to bring the reader an understanding of the innermost secrets and mysteries of Voodoo. But, before taking you on visits to eerie midnight ceremonies, it is necessary to provide explanations of some of the elements and outward manifestations of Voodoo—many totally alien to white culture—so that you can better understand the meaning of what you will see and read.

The origin of the Voodoo rites has necessarily two aspects: the rites proceed on the one hand from a supernatural origin, and on the other hand from a geographical origin. All aspects of the ritual must above all be considered secondary to the idea of the word *Voodoo* itself, which is sometimes spelled *vo-dou* or *vo-du,* since *everything* essential to the knowledge of the mystery is implicit in this word. The clearest explanation of this essential idea is that *vo* means "introspection" and *du* means "into the unknown." Consequently, the rituals form the sum total of this introspection; that is, they are the studied accomplishments that proceed from psychological information. Those who indulge in this introspection into the *mystère* (mystery) will comprehend not only the Voodoo gods, but also the souls of those who are the adepts and the servants of these gods. This is the only way in which the fruitful practice of the rites is possible to produce supernaturally extraordinary phenomena or magic.

The Voodoo rites, derived from the supernatural, proceed from the influence of the sun in the atmosphere. It would be difficult to enlarge upon this fundamental principle of Voodoo since not everyone is endowed with the ability to comprehend the esoterics of magic. Nevertheless, the effects of this supernatural agency can be observed during the course of Voodoo services, for every trained observer will fully appreciate a spectacle whose entire ceremonial pivots upon certain cult attributes that symbolize the sun.

The simplest and easiest proof that the sun is the axis upon which the entire Voodoo cult turns is the revelation that the principal attribute of solar magic is the post or pole that supports the center of the roof of the structure known as the *peristyle* of the *oum'phor,* the Voodoo temple. The peristyle is the covered gallery of thatch or corrugated iron adjoining the holy of holies or *oum'phor* proper. The roof is supported by a wooden centerpost, called the *poteaumitan,* which means to the initiates "solar support." This post is the axis of the rites. Everything in Voodoo rites has reference ultimately to the center-post. The post is an architectural representation of the chief Voodoo god *Legba.* The wood of the post denotes Mercury, the offspring of the sun and the god of the vegetable kingdom and shows that Mercury is at the same time the staff of Legba. Upon this staff the two serpents of the oum'phor must normally mount so as to be harmonized or be reunited by Mercury. Consequently, the central post of the Voodoo peri-styles is decorated with a spiral band of various colors symbolizing not only the colors of the rainbow but also the serpent gods *Danbhalah* and *Aida Wédo*. Furthermore, this sacred wood represents the structural material of the Temple of Jerusalem—the wood of Lebanon.

Near this post is kept the symbol of the moon, the Voodoo goddess *Erzulie*. This lunar symbol—a model boat—is suspended in the air from the ceiling to complete the significance of the planetary origin of the rites.

In the practice of Voodoo magic, a lighted candle is often substituted for the post and the boat is represented by ritual water.

The Voodoo pantheon of gods is composed of *loas* (gods) that come from all parts of Africa. Tradition has it that the term *vo-du* is drawn from the language of the Fons. Other tribes that contributed Voodoo gods were the Nago people, the Ibos, Congos, Dahomeans, Senegalese, Haoussars, Caplaous, Mandinges, Mondongues, Angolese, Libyans, Ethiopians, and the Malgaches. Moreover, the names of these tribes generally serve to designate separate Voodoo rites themselves. For example, to serve the Mondongue gods, the Mondongue rite is followed, which, although it does not differ basically and fundamentally from the other rites, nevertheless appears superficially different. To serve the Ibo gods, the Ibo rite is celebrated. And this rite too is fundamentally related to the other rites although it may appear different. The Pethro rite, however, which belongs to another "nation" of Voodoo loas, is different from the other rites, being more of a fire ritual. And the rite par excellence is the Ra-Da or Rada—"the royal rite of the sun." Each rite has its distinctive characteristics, although all rites generally speaking arise from the same source, have the same origin, and are completely integral.

The Voodoo rituals of the various tribes of Africa were commingled and modified as a result of the institution of slavery. Imagine, for example, a group of Aradas and of Ibos sold into slavery together. Either they had to combine their separate rites or else the dissimilarity of their rituals would impose upon them a cruel and mutual isolation in the heart of the new community to which the slave trade took them. The result of such tribal fusion was that the two different religious groups more or less combined their beliefs, thereby creating in the new slave community a Voodoo rite which to this day is not "pure."

Nevertheless, the members of certain tribes, however dispersed they may have been by the slave trade, were able (1) to regroup themselves despite wind and tide and preserve their own rites intact, or (2) maintain the purity of their rites even while living in the midst of other tribes. For this reason true descendants of the Mondongues can still be found extant throughout Haiti, in whose midst are also found Peulh or Bambara elements. They have preserved their rite intact, as well as its true interpretation, despite racial intermingling.

The ritualism of Haitian Voodoo is, then, very diverse, and its distribution over regional zones of influence is a difficult and subtle matter. However, despite this diversity, all the rites are in complete agreement as to their chief gods and their practice of magic. *Legba,* unmistakably, is their solar prototype, the magical archetype, to the science and control of whom all the rituals have reference. All the rituals include Legba as the god who "opens the gate." Without him all magic is problematical if not actually unfeasible. A ritual commences with a chanted invocation to Papa Legba, the opening words of which are: *"Papa Legba, Ouvri barrie pou nous passer* (Open the way for us to pass)."

Voodoo sinks its roots of origin in the most brilliant and most remote civilizations. The Haitian Voodooist Her-Ra-Ma-El wrote in his book *The Daimons of the Voodoo Cult:* "It is in vain that subtle processes have been employed to envelop in darkness the brilliant phases of the mental evolution of the Negro. Indisputably the antique Ethiopian-Egyptian-Assyrian civilization should be credited to its account. For thousands of years before the advent of Christ, Negro theologians and philosophers working together had organized types of academies dedicated to the study of the problems of the physical world and human destiny. All the theocratic legislation of Moses, that is, the social and religious codes contained in the Bible, bear the imprint of the sacred formulas of the Negro faith. . . ."

"The formation of the idea of religion implies beliefs about the formation of the world, about the soul, and about death. . . . Patient observations of celestial space and of the stars which throng the sky have given rise to that animism which holds that supernatural beings direct the movements of the stars, and from here primitive intuition has lead to contemplations productive of myth and legend. From here also arose those sciences of observation at the head of which must be placed astronomy. The entire hieroglyphic system of Egypt is based upon the symbolic connection which exists between the various beings and the cosmic forces, between the beings and the *lois* (laws) of creation."

The word *lois*, which means *laws* in French, is emphasized in the above context, inasmuch as it is more frequently spelled *loa* when used as a Voodoo term. The *lois*, (the "laws of creation") create the *loas* (animistic spirits) in visible manifestations such as plants, animals, and men, but chiefly as ancestors, because Voodoo is essentially a cult of ancestor worship. The Africans, believing that the *manes* (souls) of the dead reascend to the heavens, identified them with the stars. For this reason Her-Ra-Ma-El continues, "The beliefs about the soul and about death have naturally given rise to the Cult of the Dead, which in turn leads to the deification of human souls. Souls thus deified, or, as it were, canonized after death used to be called *daimons* by the Greeks. All of these manifestations of religious feeling have not failed to create a body of rites and cult ceremonies, together with appropriate symbols, or to employ all manner of paraphernalia likely to capture the popular imagination, a necessary factor in the recruiting of the greatest possible number of neophytes."

Our attention is thus fixed upon the practical process that, proceeding from the invisible to the world of men, has lead the Voodoo adepts to the rites of magic. As far as the Voodoo rites themselves are concerned, the supernatural origin of the process is the same. It now remains to consider by what accident or by what extraordinary series of occurrences the Voodoo rites were carried over to Haitian soil.

The slave trade extended from the coasts of Africa to both American continents. All the Antilles were deluged with blacks from the holds of the slave ships. They were scattered throughout the United States, but particularly in the Deep South. Brazil received a large number, as did the island of Hispaniola, which later became Haiti. The enforced immigration of black slaves from all the various African tribal populations—Anmines, Fons, Dahomeans, Yoroubas, Congos, Senegalese, and Sudanese—became inconceivably confused. In transplanting these disinherited black Africans among the colonists, the whites refused to believe that they would retain an unquenchable

faith in their gods. However, there occurred something approaching
the miraculous; for, even in irons and bound to the colonial planta-
tions, the transplanted blacks invoked not only their own gods, but
began patiently to install various Voodoo rites other than their own
in the lands of their bondage. Thus a curious moral consequence of
the slave trade was the exaltation of the African religion by an increase of faith in the Voodoo divinities.

The Voodoo rites originally derived from Africa spread to Haiti, to
Cuba, to Brazil, and even to sections of the United States. The African
ritual areas of Voodoo in Haiti extend north, south, east, and west, as
also in the Dominican Republic, and from one end of Cuba to the
other. All the islands of the West Indies have such areas: the Bahamas,
Guadeloupe, Martinique, Jamaica, Puerto Rico, the Bermudas, and
Trinidad. And in the United States, Voodoo is practiced in Florida
and the regions surrounding Charleston, New Orleans, and Galveston.

The ritual areas of the Voodoo cult in Haiti, according to information collected in the field by Odette Mennesson-Rigaud, are the
following: the Nago populations generally inhabit the north, though
not exclusively, and their ritual is more or less pure. The Ibos tend
to live in the southwest. The Congos, protecting their ritual insofar
as possible from any alteration, have preferred to reestablish themselves between the Artibonite valley and the northwest, and in the
south in the valley of Jacmel. The Dahomeans are found in the
vicinity of Gonaives, in the same region as the Congo tribes. The
Anmine or Mina tribes are in the Artibonite. The Mondongues prefer
Léogane and its environs in the southwest. The Mandingues live generally in the north as far as Cap Haitien. The African tribe most
typical of the race, whose brilliant Rada ritual derives from the solar
tradition, is established for the most part in the region northeast of
Port-au-Prince, the Cul-de-Sac Plain. Rada (or Arada) is the tribe of
Gaou-Guinou, the Arada king, an ancestor of Toussaint L'Ouverture,
the Haitian liberator. The Arada tribe likewise produced the mother
of General André Rigaud, Toussaint L'Ouverture's rival in the South,
Her name was Rose, and she was an Arada Negress.

In the early days of black slavery in America the Voodoo priests
carried on their profession without attracting much attention. But in
time the "possessions," or mystical seizures that occurred in the slave
huts, the veiled sounds of a few conical drums, as well as the desire for
indepedence kindled even in exile by a kind of patriotism, attracted

the attention of the masters. They reacted with ferocity, prohibiting all practice of Voodoo. Slaves found in possession of any symbol of Voodoo were punished with lashings, imprisonments, hangings, and "blanchings" (flaying alive a disobedient slave by laying bare with a knife the subcutaneous white tissues). So it was that the slave system succeeded in destroying in nearly all the Haitian black people the feeling and taste for making sculptures of clay or wood—an art highly integrated in other black cultures and civilizations—to the extent that it is nearly impossible to find anywhere in Haiti a single local sculpture representing an amulet or a fetish of any kind. However, none of the punishments could extinguish that faith which the transplanted blacks kept in their Voodoo gods.

The religious struggle against Voodoo continued for at least three centuries to be waged openly by the organized whites who employed all the highest refinements of cruelty, while the blacks used every possible secret ruse to protect Voodoo. This battle for their faith resulted not only in the extreme exasperation of the Voodooists, but also convinced them of the necessity of recovering with all their might their complete independence. In the beginning, the black slaves could believe that the period of their enslavement was limited, but at length they lost this illusion and priests of Voodoo consulted the gods to learn through supernatural revelations how the religious and political battle would have to be waged in order to be won.

The Voodoo gods superintended the occult government of the African clan that formed the work force of the slave system. This government, wonderfully concealed though real, was directed by the supernatural spirits who were consulted like financial advisors for a "yes" or a "no." The colonial system itself suffered terribly as a sort of imperceptible malingering encouraged by the Voodoo gods slowed the forced work of the slaves and retarded the economy proportionately. If the native Indians chose to be completely annihilated rather than to apply themselves to clever deceptions, the Africans surreptitiously and cunningly were preparing for better days ahead, devoting themselves to the task with a determination guarded by their gods. Thus, despite the cruelty of the whites, the struggle of the blacks continued its obscure course in Haiti under the supernatural auspices of the Voodoo gods until eventually Haitian black independence was won in 1804.

The Oum'phor

The *oum'phor* is the temple of Voodoo. It closely resembles the
design used by Moses to build the Ark of the Covenant and the tabernacle as described in Exodus. It consists of a large area, covered or
uncovered, called a *peristyle*, in the middle of which is a center-post
called a *poteau-mitan*. Adjoining the peristyle on one side is a square
house that is the oum'phor proper, or holy of holies.

In the Voodoo tradition Moses was initiated into Voodoo and per-
fected his knowledge as a student of the black Midianite teacher
Râ-Gu-El Pethro (Jethro). The tradition relates that Moses became
the husband of Pethro's daughter Sephora, who bore two mulatto sons
by him: Gershom, whose name means *I dwell in a foreign country*,
and Eli-Ezer, whose name means *Help of God*. The tradition goes on
to say that Aaron and Miriam, the brother and sister of Moses, com-
plained that he never should have married a black, and so to please
them Moses finally repudiated Sephora. When Moses built the first
Hebrew temple, according to Voodooists, he planted his staff in the
place occupied by the poteau-mitan in the oum'phor. The gods of Voodoo were so angry at Moses' repudiation of Sephora and Voodoo,
according to the tradition, that they "struck Miriam with white
leprosy."

The oum'phor in Haiti is said to have retained the same form as the
one used by Pethro in the land of Midian or Ethiopia.

In the square house that is the oum'phor proper, there may be one
or more chambers. One room, called the *djévo*, is where Voodoo candidates are examined and initiated. This room represents a tomb,
because the Voodoo initiate "dies" and is reborn when he becomes
an adept of the cult.

In a large oum'phor of several chambers, each may be reserved for
the worship of a single Voodoo god, each having its own separate
altar dedicated to that god. Or, in a smaller oum'phor, all the gods
may be worshipped in a single holy of holies with several altars, each
consecrated to a particular god. A colored hanging may be used to
separate the holy of holies chamber into two parts: an antichamber

and the place of worship itself. On the interior walls of the oum'phor there are elaborate ritual designs called *vèvès*.

The Pe

The altar or altar stone in a Voodoo temple is called the *pé*. It is a square or rectangular platform raised to about the height of a man's chest. Its name comes from the Dahomey word *kpé*, meaning stone. Upon the pé are a fantastic assortment of objects related to Voodoo and its rites. These include ritual rattles, bells, thunderstones with supernatural powers, flags, magic arms, chaplets, ritual necklaces, books on occultism, and even drums. In addition there are many covered jars and pots. Some of these jars, called *pots-de-tête*, contain by magic part of the spirits of the people who worship at the oum'phor. Other jars are *govis* into which the Voodoo gods descend for consultation when called.

At the heart of the Voodoo religion is the sacred serpent *Danbhalah Wédo Yé-H-we*, and in earlier times the altar was constructed with a hollow interior as a dwelling place for a live snake whose body was inhabited by the god. Today few oum'phors literally harbor a serpent, and in those that do the snake no longer is kept inside the pé but lives in a hole in the ground or in a place prepared for it. Today when Danbhalah is called, he comes to dwell briefly in a govi on the altar.

The Peristyle

The peristyle is the partly enclosed and usually roofed courtyard adjacent to the holy of holies of the oum'phor. It is the place were the elaborate mass ceremonies and rituals of Voodoo are performed, and it also is the place where the sick usually are treated.

The floor is of beaten earth and is never paved or tiled. A low wall four to five feet tall borders the peristyle. Curious spectators who are not well known at the oum'phor, or persons not properly dressed for the occasion, may stand behind the wall and still see what goes on in the peristyle without making themselves too conspicuous.

There are benches in the peristyle on which members of the oum'-phor may sit. Often a small ship model hangs from one of the crossbeams of the peristyle roof—the ritual symbol of Voodoo's most important goddess, *Erzulie*. Other objects hanging from the crossbeams include calabashes, baskets, oriflammes, and *laiers,* a kind of woven tray.

The Haitian oum'phor always has a picture of the president of the country displayed in the peristyle. This practice probably derives from the fact that African kings held their offices by divine right of the Voodoo gods, but it also serves to soften the enforcement of legal restrictions against Voodoo. On the occasion of large ceremonies garlands of small flags are hung from the crossbeams of the peristyle roof. These flags bear the red and blue colors and the arms of the Haitian republic.

A perpetual fire burns in the oum'phor yard in the center of which is planted an iron bar, traditionally fallen from the sky as a symbol of cosmic sexual desire. This bonfire is called the *forge of the Ogous* and has considerable ritual significance.

The Poteau-mitan

In the exact center of the peristyle is its most important feature—the center-post, or *poteau-mitan.* All important Voodoo ceremonies revolve around this post, the top of which is considered the *center of the sky* and the bottom of which is the *center of hell.*

The post itself is usually square and it is set into a circular pedestal of masonry. Around the side of the pedestal, or *socle,* there are triangular niches. The pedestal may be constructed of two or three concentric steps, or even of a single step. The pedestal is a form of pé, or altar, on which sacrifices to the gods may be placed.

The entire length of the post from floor to ceiling is decorated with a spiral design representing two serpent-gods: Danbhalah Wédo and Aida Wédo, the latter of which represents all the knowledge of the gods. The colors of this decoration vary from one oum'phor to another depending upon the rites an gods served by it members.

The wooden post itself represents the chief god of Voodoo—*Legba Ati-Bon,* whose name means *wood of justice.*

Hung on the side of the center-post is a whip. This whip symbolizes the obligation of penitence as well as redemption from penitence. Its spirit is implicit in the recreation of the material of the ritual sacrifice offered to the gods in propitiation, and it represents the occult sense of the command, magical or otherwise. Thus, the whip stands for both faith in and mastery of Voodoo.

The post is placed in the center of the peristyle because it is the *cosmic axis of Voodoo magic*. In conjunction with the *horizontal* of its socle, the poteau-mitan, as the *vertical*, forms a cross, whose peripheral dimensions make regularly and magically the *perfect square*. This geometric perfection maintained in every peristyle leads to its being considered the Master of Magic.

Actually, the peristyle forms geometrically the following (1) the *mitan*, or center—the non-dimensional point; (2) the rectangle, or lengthened square; (3) the circle; (4) the triangle; (5) the straight, horizontal line; (6) the spiral; (7) the curved, horizontal line; (8) the round, vertical line; (9) the square, vertical line; (10) the perfect square; (11) the cross, or intersecting straight lines; (12) the equilateral and the isosceles triangle, formed by the beams which secure the post to the roof.

This geometric scheme carries out the Voodoo belief that the serpent-god Danbhalah corresponds to the Grand Cosmic Architect, or Great Architect of the Universe, who is the Grand Master of Magic —demonstrating that the chief god is first of all a geometrician.

There are exceptions to the location of the poteau-mitan in the very center of the peristyle. I have even seen a few peristyles with two posts dividing the peristyle area into three equal parts. Elsewhere, in the region of Gonaives in northwest Haiti, I have even seen the post located not in the center of the peristyle, but rather in the center of the oum'phor proper.

There is this to remember: a Voodoo temple may even have no *visible* poteau-mitan, but will have, nevertheless, an *invisible* one. This is true in the case of the remarkable Dahomean oum'phor of La Souvenance. The peristyle—one of the largest, if not the largest I have seen—has a roof supported on all sides by two rows of posts inside and out, forming a double colonnade. Inside, the poteau-mitan is purposely replaced by a raised decagonal figure nailed to the exact center of the ceiling, making a star-shaped ceiling!

The Tree Reposoirs

The trees in the yard of the oum'phor are called *reposoirs*, or *arbres-reposoirs*. They serve as sanctuaries for the gods. The gods abide in them permanently, and the trees themselves are honored as divinities. There is usually a pedestal or basin encircling the foot of the tree. Square or triangular niches are recessed into the pedestal and in them lighted candles are often placed, surrounded by consecrated food offered in sacrifice.

Frequently a snake, the symbol of Danbhalah Wédo and Aida Wédo, lives in one of the trees. Such snakes are trained to come down from the trees during ceremonies to be fed by the Voodooists.

The reposoirs are decorated and even painted with the favorite colors of the gods to whom they belong. Ritual dances frequently are held around the trees, and on such occasions the Voodoo drums are brought out of the peristyle and placed close by.

Heaps of stones also may serve the gods as reposoirs. As a rule, a Voodoo god can require any object at all to be consecrated to its use as a reposoir, even the body or the heart of an individual.

Flag bearers during a voodoo ceremony.

A voodo-sih (voodoo adept) possessed by a loa (voodoo spirit)

Ritual flag borne by a houn'sih (flag bearer).

Ritual Congo drums.

Author with houn'sih and Pethro drums.

Ritual Rada drums (also used for Danhomey ritual).

Pethro drums ritually presented to the Sun by houn'sih.

Pethro drums laid down before the Central Post.

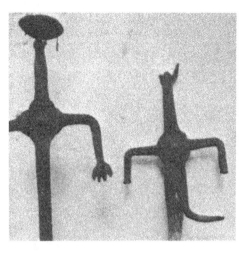

Asson (in wrought iron).

Asson and ritual hand-bell.

Ritual ogan.

Ceremonial dishes and pitchers.

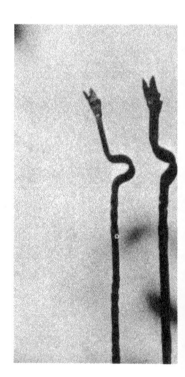

Wrought iron figures of the voodoo spirits, Danbhalah and Aïda.

Worshippers during a voodoo ceremony.

The Central Post, surrounded by voodoo diagrams.

Bull tied to the Central Post, before the sacrifice.

Houn'gan (voodoo priest)
saluting the loa Legba.

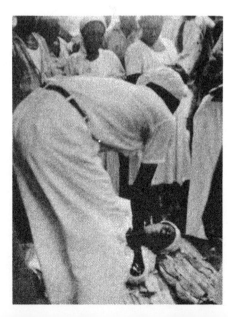

Traditional bag of Legba, hung up
on a temporary altar tree.

Ceremonial dishes for Maraça spirits.

Inner part of a oum'phor. The ship of Agoueh is on the wall.

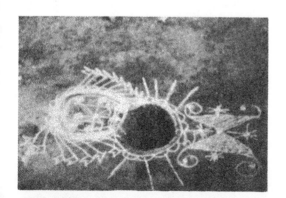

Ceremonial diagram (vèvè) drawn around the hole in which the sacrifice will be buried.

Houn'gan officiating in the oum'phor yard.

The traditional ship of Erzulie.

Rada drums hung from the ceiling of the voodoo peristyle.

2

Priests and Priestesses of Voodoo

UNLIKE other established religions, there is no heirarchy of bishops, archbishops, cardinals, or a pope in Voodoo. Each oum'phor is a law unto itself, following the traditions of Voodoo, but modifying and changing the ceremonies and rituals in various ways. This is because the religious leaders of the oum'phor speak directly with the gods of Voodoo, and are not obliged to answer to anyone else to interpret what the gods tell them. Thus, the structure of Voodoo can best be understood by the layman if he would consider how similar and how different each individual Roman Catholic church would be if for thousands of years each priest had been free to interpret Christianity as he saw fit without any intervention by Rome.

Each oum'phor has two organizational structures; one for the religious leaders, and the other for the lay members. The man or woman who is the chief religious leader of a Voodoo temple is considered royalty. If a man, the emperor of the oum'phor is called a *houn'gan*. If a woman, the empress of the oum'phor is called a *mam'bo*. Their symbol of office is the *asson*, a calabash rattle. Following are the other roles in the religious structure of the oum'phor.

31

The apprentice houn'gan or mam'bo is called the *confiance* or *mam'bo caille.*

The superintendent of the oum'phor is the *houn'guénicon caille.*

The chorus leader is the *houn'guénicon peristyle.*

The person in charge of separating and distributing the portion of sacrificial food not reserved for the gods is called the *houn'guénicon quartier-maître.*

The master of ceremonies for the Voodoo rites is called *la place.*

The person who plays a musical instrument called the *ogan* is the *ogantier.* The musician who play the triangle is the *trianglier.*

The Voodoo drummers as a group are called *houn'tôrguiers;* but each has a title—*manmanier, secondier,* and *boulahier.*

The person in charge of preserving order during services and insuring silence while the houn'gan or mam'bo works is called the *reine silence.*

The person who acquires animals to be sacrificed is the *houn'sih ventailleur.* And the person who cooks the sacrificed offerings is the *houn'sih cuisinière.*

The members of the ritual chorus who have been fully initiated in Voodoo are called *houn'sihs.*

Those who may or may not have been initiated but who have not yet been fully refashioned by the Voodoo gods are called *houn'sih bossales.*

Surrounding the oum'phor as a kind of social annex and mutual aid enterprise is the local Voodoo Society. It has officers with titles like those of a national government. It has a president, ministers, senators, deputies, generals, a secretary of state, and district and local commanders.

The Voodoo Societies organize festivities that are partly Voodoo, partly secular. They lend assistance to sister-societies. They maintain a mystical solidarity established in the Voodoo social body from the beginning of the tradition. Their true traditional function is to alleviate the sufferings, moral as well as physical, of their members, to attend to their wounds, both physical and metaphysical, to protect their members, to punish the guilty, and to bury the dead whose close relatives are unable to do so. However, this half-mystical, half-social tradition of mutual aid has lost much of its old-time effectiveness and close observance.

The Houn'gan and the Mam'bo

The role of the houn'gan or mam'bo goes beyond every definition and every ordinary conception of it. To better judge the role of these emperors and empresses of Voodoo, one should not compare them to the priests or priestesses of any other religion. Instead, their role can only be compared to that of the Pope in Roman Catholicism. On first consideration, the comparison seems daring and exaggerated; but, all things considered, the comparison is not extravagant inasmuch as, while the Roman pope's area of jurisdiction is far more extensive than that of any houn'gan, according to the voodoo cabal the houn-'gan is also etymologically a "pope," or a "papa," and that is why he is traditionally called "papa," or "papa-loa." For the same reason every priestess, or "mam'bo," is called "manman" (mama).

The authority of the houn'gan and the mam'bo is all the greater and all the more certain because everything they do proceeds directly from the powers of the invisible—the *loas* or *mystères*, as the gods of Voodoo are called. Their orders or their counsels are those of the loas, and, by extension, of the souls of ancestors, or *manes*, since Voodoo is a religion of ancestor worship.

Since the process that permits the soul to attain all of its intellectual power is astrological, the science of the houn'gan turns upon the stars. Therefore, a houn'gan's or a mam'bo's science is fallible only insofar as he or she does not know how to consult an invisible, or cannot, for one reason or another, enter into communion with the invisible.

In these pages we could mention a great number of houn'gans currently practicing in Haiti. Some of them have a certain amount of ability; however, many others have only mediocre magical power. This leads to two situations that are bad for Voodoo. First, for some time there has been far too great a number of houn'gans because life in Haiti offers people too few other rewarding careers. Consequently, initiates to the lower grades of voodoo are too often tempted to "take the asson" (the traditional expression for "becoming a houn'gan"), because this profession is rather lucrative and much respected by the people. Secondly, as a result these houn'gans and mam'bos, far too numerous as they are, often are overly prone to conform to new standards imposed upon them by the perpetual struggle between Voodoo and hostile foreign religions or the political power that aids them. This produces a syncretism of a low order to which too many oum'phors have surrendered either for purposes of immediate interests or out of cowardice, in fear of the political authority that has closed one or another oum'phor at the demand of the foreign clergy.

Consequently the supernatural gifts which the loa-ancestors confer upon the initiates of Voodoo become fewer or diminish in magical power because the manes, when confronted by such offenses against the orthodox tradition become angry, and one after the other withdraw to Africa, abandoning Haiti to itself. This is how houn'gans or mam'bos sometimes lose their powers, even fall ill, and, without making rigid sacrifices, are unable to regain their positions.

The Voodoo mystères require much greater skill and seriousness from the houn'gan and the mam'bos than they do from the rest of the people since all Haitians, in accordance with the tradition of the loas, are magically placed under the jurisdiction of the Voodoo priests. The slightest failure on the part of the priests injures not only those subject to this jurisdiction but the mystères themselves, because the uninitiated as well as the enemies of the cult are always on the lookout for false indications of its ineffectiveness or indeed of its demonism.

The Voodoo houn'gan or mam'bo is the confessor, doctor, magician, confidential advisor to individuals and to families, to politicians, and even financial advisor to people of highest as well as those of lowest estate. He is a prophet, too, of such a sort that scarcely anything is done without his advice in the community where he is the central figure. In the oum'phor he presides over everything that is done. Here his authority is absolute.

The amount of his knowledge is truly astonishing. The moment his own knowledge fails, he consults the loas in order to increase it. However, it is not only by summoning the loas that he is able to see them. He also often beholds them in dreams or by a supernatural percipient ability based upon sciences such as palmistry, fortune-telling by cards, fire, water, or figure-drawings, in which he is often an expert.

The houn'gan or the mam'bo leans upon the *pé* or altar when, shut up in the oum'phor, he or she calls the loas into the *govi* (a jar into which the mystères descend when called). The loas enter these receptacles from which they may then speak not only with houn'gan but even with any who happen to be present. However, the "papa" secludes himself in the chamber that serves as the holy of holies, and it is there, out of sight even of the initiates, that he asks the loas to come down into the govi. He accomplishes this by certain traditional magic words that, to the persistent rhythm of the asson, attract the mystères from the astral zones of the invisible.

The Asson

The *asson*, the calabash rattle that is the symbol of office of the houn'gan or mam'bo, usually is called a ritual rattle by ethnologists. In any case, the asson is a calabash taken from the *calebassier courant* tree, which is the tree-reposoir par excellence of the great mystère Danbhalah-Wédo. The *calebasse ordinaire* is pierced with a hole to receive a handle. This is called the *coua-coua*, and is used by the lesser officiants at rites other than the Pethro. The *calebasse courante* has a natural handle. The *coua-coua* is the asson of the Pethro rite. While the *calebasse courante* grows on a liana, the *calebasse ordinaire* grows on a tree, the *crescentia cujete (bignoniaceae)*.

It may be noted that the solar tradition of the great invisibles of Ethiopia ascribes the *calebassier courant* to Danbhalah as his reposoir, while Haitian initiates follow an altered version of orthodox teaching which holds that the *calebasse ordinaire* climbs upon the essence (i.e. the tree) consecrated to the mystère. There is sometimes controversy in Voodoo over this kind of adaptation of symbols. For example, whereas the solar tradition attributes the boat to Erzulie (the Virgin), in Haitian oum'phors the boat is made the magical attribute of Agoueh, the marine husband of Erzulie.

The houn'gan or the mam'bo traditionally holds the asson in his hand, along with the *clochette*, or bell, which represents the magic powers of the Occident, or Ethiopia. The asson is held between the right thumb and index finger; the bell between the ring-finger and the second finger.

The fruit of the *calebassier courant* and the *calebassier ordinaire* has been chosen as an attribute and a symbol of command, because, it reflects geometrically the *magic principle*, that is, the elevation or the assumption of the raw material of the sacrifices which propitiants deposit ritually upon the socle of the poteau-mitan. The asson or *cale-*

basse courante makes a perfect geometric symbol in that by itself—its metaphysical symbol being the abyss and chasm—it represents a sphere or perfect circle; furthermore, it grows its own handle, a fact which, in the symbolic geometric, signifies that the calabash itself is controlled by the straight line formed by the handle.

In reality, by the sphere or the circle, plus the handle which symbolizes the poteau-mitan or the vertical, the asson becomes a *geometric synergy* combining the two activating principles of all magic: the magic wand, which is the handle, and the magic circle.

Inside the asson are stones and the vertebrae of snakes which give the asson its sound. These stones and vertebrae are considered bones of the African ancestors worshipped in Voodoo. So the bones and vertebrae make the calabash a musical instrument for ritual power. When the asson "speaks," the sacred spirits of the ancestors appear. In Africa, the snake whose vertebrae are used to symbolize the ancestors is the Royal Python, which represents the eternity of life. The stones inside the asson are of eight different kinds to represent eight different ancestor-gods and are of eight different colors since the eight means eternity.

Therefore, the sound of the asson represents magically the powers of the ancestors from whom Voodoo is handed down. This element of the orthodox tradition is the vertebra of the snake, since the mystère *Danbhalah Wédo* is supposedly the oldest of the ancestors, and because the snake is *Da* or *Dan, Dam, Don,* or *Dom.* The vertebrae, which are carefully strung in accordance with a special magical rite followed in preparing the asson, represent *all the astral powers* or *all the powers of ancestors* who are *identified with the stars,* at the head of which the Sun (Legba) and the Moon (Erzulie) magically preside.

Furthermore, the asson is surrounded with a network of porcelain beads of all colors. These beads, too, have a certain significance: they represent all the atmospheric powers of Erzulie, that is to say, all the powers of the *solar prism* consolidated color-wise by the symbol of the *mystère Erzulie on the "point-couleuvre-Aida-Wédo"*—the rainbow.

Owing to all of these geometric, chromatic, and magical virtues, the asson is considered the traditional image of the Orient. Prepared correctly, it should contain all the magic powers of the Orient. And inasmuch as the Orient, in practical magic, is the *master of the astral,* the asson has under its command all the *loas* or *occult powers of the astral ancestors* which we shall presently discover under the forms of the Voodoo *vèvès* or ceremonial diagrams. For this reason one may see the houn'gan strike these ritual designs: *he strikes the vèvès with the asson to release the astral power and then to utilize it.*

Taking the Asson

In Voodoo, the place in Africa where the spirits abide is the astral city of Ifé; and in Haiti the place where the Voodoo ancestral spirits have come to dwell since the days of slavery is La Ville Aux Camps. In Ifé, therefore the city of the Voodoo spirits' origin, resides the totality of magic powers personified by the mystère Danbhalah. So it is natural that for a person to acquire the magic powers of Voodoo, ritually enacted in the *prise d'asson* or "asson-taking" ceremony, the candidate for the Voodoo priesthood must go and take the asson at Ifé in Africa by traveling logically via the line of the center-post that traverses the asson's magic circle.

The center-post is therefore called by its analogical surname of *Papa Loko Ati-sou Poun'goueh*, so named because the recipient must traverse the waters of the abyss *(poun'goueh)* in order to reach Africa in the vertical direction of the celestial city, Miître Grand Bois. Therefore, by analogy and homophony, the future houn'gan is taken by his initiators, older houn'gan, to a large wooded place *(grand bois* in French, *phazoun* in African). He is brought here to receive the asson; then he is lead to another kind of "large wood," namely the wooden cross of Baron Samedi, lord of the cemetery, to obtain the latter's approval.

In any event, just as the whole system of the *pé* has changed while the old principle has been retained in the *govi*, the ritual prescribed for candidates for the asson is very complex. It is complex because, like initiation into the Masonic Lodge, it partakes more of the nature of an initiatory examination than of an occult performance. It is to the interest of the initiating houn'gans to increase the elaborateness of the essential ritual by multiplying its complexities, thereby lining their own purses.

Since our purpose is to describe the true, original, revealed Voodoo, we shall omit all discussion of these complexities—even though their spectacular charm is certainly undeniable—in order to set forth the

secret of the original ceremonial. This is the requisite ceremonial for
creating a new houn'gan, that is to say, for conferring upon him
supernatural powers by means of the asson, provided, of course, that
the houn'gans participating as initiators are true descendants of the
authentic line whose first member was Dan Gbé himself, lord of the
astral.

The future houn'gan presents himself to an older houn'gan, the
authentic representative of the ancestors or of the serpent-ancestor,
and requests that the office of houn'gan be conferred upon him. If
the candidate is already a houn'gan's apprentice, and is accordingly
a member of his oum'phor, he requests his teacher to confer the asson
upon him. The older houn'gan requests the assistance of two other
houn'gans—the oldest he can find—by virtue of the esoteric prescrip-
tion that holds that three masons together form a regular lodge. However, he may be assisted by six houn'gans, thus forming a solar or perfect lodge.

The houn'gan in charge requires the candidates to spend a period of
purification in a chamber adjoining the oum'phor proper, called the
djévo, the chamber from which initiates into the voodoo cult make
their entrance. The period of purification is determined, or should be,
in principle, by the occult number of the mystère whose "point" the
houn'ior, or candidate, is couché, or "put to bed." If the candidate is
couché upon the "point" of Legba, the period is seven days; if of Erzulie, six days. The couché of the houn'ior corresponds to the prostra-
tion of the cardinals at St. Peter's, in Rome. The cardinals lie prostrate
(couché) for a ceremony in the course of which they receive the cardinal hat. In Haiti, a houn'ior "put to bed" upon the "houn'gan-point,"
remains twenty-one days in the djévo, which corresponds to the virtues of the Solar Seven multiplied by the Three of the Holy Trinity.

After the purification in the djévo, the houn'gan, in a kind of litany
of the saints, invokes all the Voodoo mystères, the assisting houn'gan
giving the responses. Part of the initiation ceremony follows:

First houn'gan:

Ma'p di ou bonjou,	I bid you good morning,
Papa Legba Ati Bon Kata- rouleau;	Papa Legba Ati Bon Data-rou- leau;
ma'p di ou bonjou,	I bid you good morning,

Papa Loko Ati Dan Poun'- Papa Loko Ati Dan Poun'goueh
goueh Ibo Loko;   Ibo Loko;
ma'p di ou bonjou,   I bid you good morning,
Papa Danbhalah Wédo;   Papa Danbhalah Wédo;
ma'p di ou bonjou,   I bid you good morning,
Papa Ogou, Ogou-Fer, Ogou   Papa Ogou, Ogou-Fer, Ogou
Chango;   Chango;
ma'p di ou bonjou,   I bid you good morning,
Afrique Guinin Tocan Da-   Afrique Guinin Tocan Dahoumin.
houmin.

Before speaking the houn'gan orients and casts some water to the
four cardinal points. Then, pointing out the candidate for the asson,
he says:

Main X, cé pitit ou qui   Behold X, he is your child who
vlé ou; li di cé pitit ou,   desires you; he says he is your
Afrique Tocan. Aida Wédo   child,
Tocan Dahoumin, cé tout   Afrique Tocan. Aida Wédo
Guinin   Tocan Dahoumin, he is com-
li yé. Li cé cheval Marassah, pletely African,
Tocan Fréda Wédo.   he is. He is the Marassah's horse,
                            Tocan Fréda Wédo.

Response:

Li di cé pitit ou,   He says he is your child,
Afrique Tocan. Aida Wédo   Afrique Tocan. Aida Wédo
Tocan Dahoumin, cé tout   Tocan Dahoumin, he is com-
Guinin   pletely African,
li yé. Li cé cheval Marassah, he is. He is the Marassah's horse,
Tocan Fréda Wédo.   Tocan Mreda Wédo.

The officiating houn'gan again orients and casts water on the
ground, saying:

Djo-là passée . . .   The water has been passed through . . .

Response:

Djo-là passée . . .   The water has been passed through . . .

The future houn'gan is then possessed by a loa. The officiant continues:

Cé lan Guinin nous yé . . .   We are in Africa . . .

Drunk with the loa who has "mounted" * him, the future houn'gan

* The person who is "mounted" is called a *cheval,* or "horse" of the god.

replies:

Ma'p suivé ou, Papa moin . . . (I will follow you, my Father . . .)

The future houn'gan is obliged to recline upon the ground, entirely naked and wearing no jewelry of any kind. Sometimes his head is shaved. He prays to the Voodoo spirit for the remission of all his sins, and swears an oath to consecrate himself as a priest to the service of the loas and never to reveal anything whatever about the initiation. The oldest houn'gan sprinkles him with holy water and raw clairin, and leads him to the *pé.* There he is at Ifé. Totally possessed by the guiding spirit, he staggers, supported by the old houn'gan, who makes him bow down before the stone of the *pé* from which the mystère Dan Gbé Tò bestows upon him the asson and the bell.

Outside the *djévo* the battery of drums, appropriate to the rite in which the ceremony is being performed, resounds. The chorus of houn'sihs sings the ritual chants "sent" by the hounguénicon. At this point the newly initiated, "mounted" by the spirit, takes over the service. He is now a houn'gan, because, having "passed through the water" he went to Ifé, where Dangbé delivered to him the asson at the request of the old houn'gans, the custodians of the Voodoo tradition.

For various reasons, Dan-G-Bé sometimes refuses to give the asson. In such cases the petitioner frequently uses the asson anyway, despite the Spirit's refusal. Nevertheless, he is a false houn'gan, and there are certain operations in which he is successful only because he employs devices stolen from authentic houn'gans. The Voodoo tradition holds that such a candidate "did not go under the water" *(li pas té allé en bas d'leau).*

In the Voodoo tradition, Moses had a Pethro asson and related its secrets to the rabbis. The name of the Voodoo asson is *koheleth-a-dam,* *koheleth-a-dom, koheleth-a-don,* or *koheleth-a-dan.* The Voodoo tra-

dition explains the initiatory formula through the general meaning of
the book of Ecclesiastes (12, 13): "Fear God, and keep his command-
ments." The formula is Coeleth, Cò-Lè-Th, Cò-Lé-Tha, or Koheleth
(the Preacher). Inasmuch as the book of Ecclesiastes is the Second
Book of Solomon or the Second Book of Wisdom, Voodoo tradition
considers it the magic of the Temple of David, a Negro king, of
Solomon, his son, and the basis of the magic tradition of the oum'phor.
The *koléthadan* or Voodoo asson reveals by its authority that man
is dependent not upon himself but upon the superhuman occult forces
called by Voodoo initiates *mystères*, *angels*, *saints*, or *loas*, according
to the region in which the Voodoo religion is practiced.

The following is the best explanation of the entire formula:

coeleth: cabalistic wisdom or discipline; the tradition of the
clergy and the church; *a-:* Grand Master; the square or alpha;
dan: the serpent, traditionally represented by Danbhalah.

For this reason the serpent in the universal tradition is the animal
that initiates man and woman, like the serpent that descended from
the tree of knowledge to initiate Eve and Adam, (whose name is
found in the *a-dam* of the formula *koheleth-a-dam*), the same serpent
that descends from the center-post of the peristyle to initiate the
houn'sih-canzos, the houn'iors, the houn'gans, the mam'bos, the houn'-
guénicons, and others.

The formula indicates also the assembly or gathering of Voodoo
initiates in the peristyle of the oum'phor, referred to in a ritual chant
that calls them together at the beginning of the ceremonies:

La fanmi semblé; en é o;
   la fanmi semblé, non;
E Agouèto, ça hin'dé;
   na'pé hin'dé o;
   la fanmi semblé; en é o;
   na'pé hin'dé Papa Loko Ati-sou.

La fanmi semblé; en é o;
   na'pé hin'dé Grande Aizan
   Vélékété.
La fanmi semblé; en é o;
   la fanmi semblé, non,

Come together, family, en é o;
   come together, now, family;
E Agouèto, that's the call;
   we shall call, O;
   come together, family, en é o;
   we shall call Papa Loko Ati-
   sou.

Come together, family, en é o;
   we shall call Grande Aizan
   Vélékété.
Come together, family, en é o;
   come together, now, family,

E Agouètò, Gouètò, ça hin'dé;   E Agouètò, Gouètò, that's the call;
   na hin'dé Marassah Do-sou,   we shall call the Marassah Do-
                                         sou,
Do-sah, Do-goueh.   Do-sah, and Do-goueh.
E Agouètò! Ou ça hin'dé you vrai! E Agouètò! You can really call
                                      them!

In closing this chapter a word must be said about one of the most
extraordinary facts concerning Voodoo. If the officiants at an initiation are themselves unable to give correct and complete instruction
to an apprentice, the mystères themselves give the instruction by
"mounting" someone, who then instructs the initiate verbally. Otherwise the mystères send him dreams or visions when necessity arises.
A great many houn'gans are created in this supernatural manner. It
is the loas themselves who initiate them and give them the asson.

3

Gods and Goddesses of Voodoo

THE adepts of Voodoo, relying upon the fundamentals of the African tradition, believe the place of origin of Voodoo was Ifé, the name of a legendary city whose replica actually exists in Yoruba in southern Nigeria. At the same time, Ifé is a mystical city from which comes the greatest of the Voodoo *mystères* and it is regarded as a kind of African Mecca.

Ifé is the fatherland of the Voodoo gods. It is from here that the revelation descended into the spirit and the heart of those African Voodooists who established the religion practiced today by their descendants. The Voodoo revelation descends under the double form of the serpents Danbhalah Wédo and Aida Wédo. The serpents represent the African *Almighty*—the Ancestor—Voodoo being religiously and ritually an ancestral cult in which the supreme personage is "the first of the living."

Needless to say, everything that constitutes the framework and mode of life among the earth's inhabitants springs from Ifé: administration and administrative methods, royalty, presidency of state, culture, the major and minor arts, medicine, architecture, navigation, and especially religion and religious magic, but more particularly that phase of magic called *divination*.

Since royalty is a divine right, it thereby follows that the portrait of the chief of the state, in accordance with a Haitian custom deriving from the tradition of Africa, is always hung in the place of honor in all the oum'phors, because, say the initiates, "the king is the direct representative of God."

Proceeding from the principle that every king or chief of state is the representative of God on earth, the Voodoo tradition identifies Ifé with the celestial position of the sun, and with the sun itself. Hence the king is found to be identified with the sun. The supernatural origin of the Voodoo cult is astrological in nature for Ifé is identified with the sun. Moreover, since the sun is the god *Legba*, the region of the sky where the sun rises is *Legba-Ji*, an expression bearing the general meaning "god of the Creation."

Legba, the synthetizing god of Voodoo, is the Orient, the East, the chief cardinal point, the point of space which presides at or governs the magic.

The African origin of the Voodoo gods is somewhat complex, for although Legba unquestionably comes from Ifé, the whole Voodoo pantheon by no means comes from the same place. This pantheon is composed of *mystères* originating in different parts of the world: some from Dahomey, some from the Congo, others from the Nago regions, still others from the Sudan. Certain gods come from the land of the Ibos; others are by preference Pethro *mystères*, and a list of the "*nations of voodoo mystères*" would necessarily include the names of all of the tribal regions on the map of Africa: Morocco, Mauritania, Nigeria, Liberia, Cameroon, Angola, Madagascar, and many others.

It is the differences or distinctions established in Voodoo by the "nations of loas" which tend to diversify the cult by dividing it into "rites," although its fundamental integrity as well as its traditional homogeneity are completely preserved.

Contrary to general opinion, among the countries where the Voodoo *mystères* originated must be included Judea and Ethiopia, for both the Jewish and the Ethiopian cults hold their origin to be from the sun. Among the Jews, the sun is represented by a serpent upon a staff—the serpent called *Da*(vid); among the Ethiopians, the serpent is represented by a lion—*David*—the Lion of the solar house of Judah (a title preserved by the emperor of Ethiopia). In Voodoo the same serpent, likewise called *Da*, and the same lion, called *Legba*, preside at the head of the cult.

The *mystère* which bears the serpent *Da* is another serpent, Ai-Da. This second serpent is, accordingly the Virgin of Voodoo—*Aida Wédo*. As mother of the Voodoo Legba, she is the wife of the sun, that is, she is the moon. The Africans call her *Mawu*, but she is best known in Haiti as *Erzulie*.

Legba, the origin and the male prototype of Voodoo, is the sun which presides over the rites, while Erzulie, the origin and the female prototype, is the moon. Legba is the Christ; Erzulie the Virgin. The other *mystères* follow in their turn in hierarchical order.

In his outward manifestation, Legba is pictured as a man who *sprinkles water on the ground*. He is the deity recognized in those adepts who at the commencement of every ceremony sprinkle the ground with water. Erzulie is represented as a dark-skinned Ethiopian woman. She is necessarily dark since she is burned by her husband the sun. The occult aspect of this is easily understood: this woman, very dark but very beautiful, is identified, in the Afro-Judean tradition, with the very dark but very beautiful Queen of Sheba. Therefore, the serpent, Aida-Wédo, seen on the walls of the Voodoo oum'phor, is recognized through the process of religious synchretism, as the Ethiopian queen who visited Solomon, the builder of the Temple. By these illustrations the astrological origin of the Voodoo cult and its areas of religious influence throughout the world can be explained most easily.

The African tradition inherited through the Haitian oum'phors reveals that the female, or lunar, serpent Aida-Wédo seen painted on the oum'phor walls is a *path of seven colors* employed by the divine power as a medium for transmitting his orders from the sky to the earth. This path, which conducts God from the sky to the earth is, of course, the rainbow. As a symbol, the rainbow—like Voodoo—has its origin from the sun. In the oum'phor, then, Erzulie, who in the form of a rainbow plays the role of the lunar serpent Aida-Wédo, is the magic principle of wealth and prosperity. She is invoked by all who desire a change of fortune or who wish to become wealthy. The symbol of the moon which she personifies as a voodoo *mystère* is silver, while the symbol of Legba (the sun) is gold.

Legba is explained by Voodoo traditionalists as having the same origin and attributes as the Greek god Mercury—the symbol of Mercury being two serpents entwined about a staff and the symbol of Voodoo being the two serpents entwined about the center-post of the oum'phor. The traditionalists further see Christ originating in Legba, a mulatto because he is the son of the sun and the moon.

Summoning the Gods

The gods of Voodoo—the loas, mystères, or voudon—reach the place where the houn'gan or mam'bo summons them by leaving the atmospheric abode assigned them by the occult spirit referred to as the "source higher than ourselves." These gods may enter a *govi* (a pottery jar) or may become incarnate by "mounting" a Voodoo follower (the cheval, or "horse"). The cheval loses absolutely all consciousness. It is the mystère alone who acts. He prophesies, dances, and performs magic, without the person who is thus mounted knowing anything at all of what the mystère does or says. Even when the mystère has departed, the "horse" remains unaware of his actions and his movements until informed of them by a witness. The person is changed physically, insofar as that is possible, by means of gestures, expressions, the voice, clothing, tastes, age, habits, and customs of the mystère, which abolishes the very soul of the person possessed. For example, an eight-year-old child mounted by a *"Grande"* (an old woman mystère) such as Grande Erzulie, will be feeble, practically speechless and squeaking like an old woman 100 years old; while an old man 90 years old possessed by a raging Ogou such as Bacossou will bound out of his torpor, brandish his sword, and dance better than Nureyev.

After the possession, the individual usually falls into a state which, for the most part, is characterized by a complete indifference as to the god's actions during the mounting. It must be added that certain ritual possessions are very exhausting for the "horse," particularly if he is mounted by the more powerful loas. The more powerful the loas, the greater the "horse" is fatigued after the possession.

As a general rule, the personality of the "horse" is so effaced during what is traditionally called the *"crise de loa"* (loa-crisis), that even the sick who are mounted by the mystères instantly manifest a complete disregard for their illness or infirmity. It is not unusual to see a sick person who has scarcely dragged himself into the peristyle get up vigorously, after being mounted, and start to dance, to gesticulate frenetically, and even to leap.

At a Voodoo ceremony, someone in the company may be seated or

walking around when all at once he seems to receive a terrible blow
in a certain place on his body. Some initiates claim that it is at the
nape of the neck; others that it is in the legs. Often he utters a cry
or a moan, giving a clear impression that an invisible force means to
or is trying to get control of him. He struggles, staggers, nearly always going around in circles, and throws out his arms in all directions
in an obvious effort to drive off the force that is trying to possess him.

The "horse" hurls himself violently upon the company, against
whose bodies he reclines as though to implore their help. To be sure,
some people know certain signs they can make or words they can utter
to send the mystère away. But the moment the invisible power has
mounted the "horse," he becomes transformed, straightens himself
up, and goes about the business of the mystère *who has taken his
place in the person's own body*. The mystère gives his greetings, and
usually asks for his special emblems.

These emblems consist of arms, costumes, kerchiefs to tie around
the head, the waist, the wrist, or the ankles, magic wands, beverages,
and perfumes, which stand as symbols of the hermetic colors and
forms of the invisibles. The symbolism in these objects permits the
loas to perform their magic better.

The loas depart more easily than they arrive. Often they show
signs of suddenly losing interest in what they are doing, drop whatever objects they have in hand, sometimes utter a mournful cry, and
lean upon someone or slump to their knees, abandoning the physical
body of their "horse." At other times they leave their "horse" with
such ease that it is difficult to tell when they are gone, so that people
sometimes ask if the mystère is "still there." In this case one may occasionally even speak to a person believed to be still mounted, think-
ing he is addressing the mystère, when, indeed, the mystère is no
longer there. This confusion can also work the other way. Often a
person is mounted so easily that another may suddenly realize, when
talking to him, that he is talking to a loa instead.

A mystère does not necessarily have to be summoned in order to
mount a person, and often a loa who has not been called makes his
appearance. In any case, whether summoned or not, a mystère can
always be sent away either by the houn'gan or by any other person
who knows how.

From this it follows that in the oum'phors, the role of the houn'gan
or the mam'bo is to attract the loas by the water (which they call

manman bagaille-là) and by the sacrifices to the sound of the drums
and chants, but in any case by such means as they, as masters, have
at their disposal, and from the onset of the loa-crisis right up to the
moment when it may be necessary to dismiss them back into the astral or the invisible. The following is witnessed invariably after the
descent of a mystère: the mystère "mounts his horse," then at once is
obliged to salute the houn'gan or the mam'bo before concerning himself with his own proper magic in the peristyle, until he judges it time
to leave on his own accord or until the houn'gan dismisses him for
one reason or another. Occasionally the houn'gan's or the mam'bo's
knowledge is used to stabilize a possession which becomes a lamen-
table struggle in which neither "horse" nor mystère is able to get control. The water, chants, and drums play a considerable part in the
stabilization process.

Houn'gans insufficiently trained have been known to become insane
or ill, and "horses" to be terribly mistreated or even killed because
they had been overcome by the mystère whom they served. The
houn'gan who lacks sufficient knowledge to master the mystères is
exposed to terrible risks. We have personally witnessed the following
moving scene: A houn'gan who was questioning mystères in an oum-
'phor and calling them successively in a govi was not able to temper
the anger of Loco-Ati-sou. Loco struck him on the head, probably
with an object lying on the *pé*, not without first having made an in-
fernal din. The young houn'gan fell unconscious under the blow.
A deathly silence ensued. Another houn'gan who was outside with us
was obliged to use his authority and open the door of the *bagui* so as
to find the unconscious man who we being hounded by Loco. The
man was brought into the peristyle and only with great difficulty was
he brought around.

Such confrontation with a Voodoo god sometimes may even result
in the death of the houn'gan, when the initiate stands up to a *voudoun*
or disobeys his commands. They say that in such cases the mystère
"touches" them if they fall ill, and "eats" them if they die. This is not
an astonishing fact if one realizes that the power of a *voudoun* such
as Legba—according to the fundamentals of the tradition—is able to
attain a temperature of $30,000,000°$ C. in the star that represents the
town of Ifé, when it pleases the mystère to rise this high with his
"horse," and that the houn'gan would be unable to temper it. Anything can be devastated in the terrible ranges of this fantastic energy.

Theoretically we note that, if he is capable, the houn'gan is also able to cause a loa to rise to this altitude. At the same time we must admit that contemporary houn'gans no longer possess this ability. This was the case, however, when, to win the wars of Haitian independence over the armies of Napoleon which seemed invincible, the n gan [1] who were among the slaves caused certain of them to arise through the agency of the Ogous, the Marinette Bois Chèches, the Jean Pethros, and the Aloumandias. Independence once acquired, the country was devastated by water, iron, fire, and poison, from Tiburon to Maribaroux and from Môle Saint Nicolas to Grand Gosier because of the temperature to which these n'gan had carried the Dessalines, the Capoix-la-morts, and the Christophes—all of them "mounted." But this was only after the African priesthood had more or less appeased the loas who had brought to pass this epic by attaining this revolutionary temperature, unique in the history of the world —these loas to whom had been sacrificed all the agricultural and industrial riches of the metropolis in a few hours, not counting the thousands of "white heads."

We say "more or less" because up to the present the loas say that the heroes and the beneficiaries of this supernatural epic have not kept the promises which were made to them. The daily experience with Voodoo proves that it is much better to refuse the services of a voudoun than to make him promises which are never kept. For the mystère himself always keeps his promises whatever the difficulties that he must surmount.

What the Gods Can Do

A mystère can mount a person for the following reasons:

(1) To protect him.

(2) To confer upon him a power or a faculty that he needs for the successful accomplishment of a task, and which he does not ordinarily have. To permit him, for example, to swim to land in case of shipwreck, if he does not know how to swim. Many people report that such-and-such a person "did not know how to swim, and when a sailboat on which he was sailing was wrecked, naturally he almost

---

[1] *Houn'gan* is a phonetic variant of the African terms *N'gan, N'ganga, Moganga. Moganga*, for example, is applied to the fetish-makers of the Oubangui.

drowned, since the accident occurred on the open sea; however, *Agoueh* mounted him and brought him to shore."

(3) To permit him to remove himself with supernatural speed.

(4) To cure him of illness or to prevent him from suffering.

(5) To give him counsel. In this case, those who speak to the possessed person repeat to him the advice that the loa gave during the "loa-crisis."

(6) To give some other person a treatment, or simply to prescribe or to compose a remedy.

(7) To punish the "horse" for some offense. In this case, despite the commands and rebukes of the houn'gan, the mystère may refuse to leave—to dismount the "horse"—for hours or days, determined to exhaust him as much as possible. Often we see the consequences of such a punishment: a dislocated limb, or an illness which only the mystère who caused it can cure.

(8) To point out some forbidden ritual.

(9) To give warning of danger threatening an individual or the community.

(10) To preside over, or to assist at a ritual ceremony.

(11) To come and get a sacrificial offering.

Because of all these functions—relating as much to the cult as to everyday life—the most important consequences for the mystical life as well as the national life follow from the participation of the Voodoo loas in human affairs. Thus, in everything that particularly concerns Haitian life, Voodoo is like a superior soul, which acts as a counterpart of the soul as ordinarily regarded, and which accompanies man in all his occupations.

The Magic Center of Voodoo

The magic center of Voodoo is found in the center of or in the middle of the circle of the post or of the globe of the asson. For this reason the handle is fixed in the middle of the asson, and the post in the center of the masonry socle.

The mystère who magically guards the wooden part of the asson (the handle) and the wood of the center-post is called Loko Ati-Sou, whose name is derived from his magical attributes: Loko (the place)

Ati (of the wand) Sou (magic). Hence Papa Loko is not only the mystère who guards the center-post, but also the mystère who serves as treasurer of the oum'phor. Consequently he knows the best magic formulas. So, just as the "magic purity of the astral powers of the center-post" is personified by the loa called Grande Ai-Zan (which signifies "knowledge of the mysteries of the astral through the cross"), the loa Grande Aizan is called Mam'bo Aizan: the magician par excellence of the oum'phor. For this reason Grande Aizan is believed to be the wife of Loko Ati-Sou. The magic entourage of Mam'bo Aizan is composed of mystères of the African "nation" called the "A-Dan I-Zo Y-an Go Nation."

The Voodoo Pantheon

The origin of the ensemble of Voodoo gods has become extraordinarily complex both on the supernatural level and on the geographic level because of the assimilation of new gods day after day into the pantheon. Some of these new gods come from the noteworthy personalities of dead initiates whose souls have become divinities. Other new gods may come from another rite and are called "strangers to a tribal clan" or "purchased mystères." The ritual of the tribal clan which "purchases" them is complicated by the fact that each mystère has its ritual mode of behavior and its personal attributes that tend to multiply the ritual accessories and augment the ceremonial itself. For example, if, in a particular rite, the mystère *Ogou Bhalin'dio* and the mystère *Ogou Fer* are being "served," their ritual diagrams as well as their colors are different although they are of the same "family" of loas. Their ritual chants also are markedly different; wherefore it may be concluded that, although the planetary origin of these two loas is from the same sidereal source, the separate origins of their personal ceremonials render the Voodoo ritual very diverse.

The following list of mystères will give an idea of the extent of the number of Voodoo gods. It is impossible to name all the loas, especially since every day new ones are created out of the spirits of dead initiates by Voodoo priests.

Atin-Gbi-Ni-Mon-Sé (the omnipotence of Ati-G-Bô Legba)
Yé Dan-Gbé

Dan-Bha-Lah Wé-Do (Danbhalah Yé-Wé
Ai-Da Wé-Do (Ayidohwédo)
Maou-Lihsah
Lihsah (Lihsah Gba Dya)—Legba (Leh Gba Dya)
Legba Ati-n Bon (Legba Atibon)
Québiésou (Héviozo)
Grande Ai-Zan
Assatò Micho To Kpo Dounou Voudoun
A Dan Man Sih WéDo
Aganman (Caîman, Anolis)
Adya Houn'tò (the drums "mounted" by a process known as
    "à dya")
Agaou -Tonnerre
Agassou-Allah-Da
Erzulie (Maîtresse Erzulie, Grande Erzulie)
Grande Fleurizon
Ogou Fer
Ogou Bha Lin Dyo
Ogou Bha Tha Lah
Ogou Shango
Agoueh R Oyo
Azagon
Agoum (Adoum Guidi)
Aglaou Wé-Do
Agoueh-Tha Oyo
Ogou Ashadah (A Shah Deh)
Zocliman
Sim'bi Y-An-Kitha
Sim'bi Y-An Deh-Zo
Sim'bi Y-An Pha-Ca
Sim'bi Y-An-Po-Lah
Marassah (twins)
Marassah (triplets)
Marassah (quadruplets)
Avadra Bô-Roi
Grande Alouba
Grande Aloumandya
Papa Loko Azam'blo Guidi

Aroyo
Dan Hwé-Zo
Boum'ba Maza (a family of loas)
Lemba Filé Sabre
Sobo
Badè
Badè-sih Cala Houn'sou
Houn'
Houn'sih
Houn'gan
Houn'guénicon
Houn'tò
Ti Gougoune
Gougoune Dan Leh
Québiésou Dan Leh (m)
Canga
Zin'ga
Lem'bha Zaou
Man Inan
Madame Lah-Oué
Laoca
La Sirène (Erzulie)
La Baleine (Erzulie)
An Wé-Zo
Ogou Bha-Da-Gri
Zaou Pemba
Manman Pemba (a drum which is simultaneously a cannon)
O-Sou Maré
Mackandal
Silibo Vavo
Grande Sim'ba
Ti Kitha Démembré
Sim'ba Maza
A Dan Hi
Cousin Zaca
Zo
Zo Man Kilé
Sophie Badè

Agaou Comblé
Bô-Sou Trois Cornes
Jakata
Danbhalah La Flambeau
Zinclin Zain
Azaca Médeh
Houn'non'gonn' ("the place of sound," personified by Maîtresse
    Hounon'gon, an initiate who directs the ceremonies)
Ossangne
Ogou Y-Am-San
Guédé Nouvavou
Guédé Mazaca
Guédé L'orage (the Storm)
Guédé Cinq Jours Malheureux (Five Days' Misfortune)
Guédé Ti Puce lan d'l'eau (Little-Flea-in-the-Water)
Zazi Boulonnin
Ogou Can-Can Ni Can
Criminel Pethro
Pin'ga Maza
Roi Ou-Angole
Zantahi
Zantahi Médeh
Ou-An Ilé (the mother of the Dahomean King Tegbésou, after
    becoming a mystère)
Ibo Sou-Aman
Brisé Macaya
Brisé Pem'bha
Nannan Blouklou
Ibo Kiki-Lih-bô
Erzulie Taureau (The Bull)
Erzulie Fréda
Erzulie Gé Rouge (Red-Eye)
Erzulie Mapian (Louse)
Ti Pierre Dantor
Ti Jean
Ogou Ashadeh
Bossou Ashadeh (King Tegbésou of Dahomey)
Ashadeh Bòcò
Bòcò Legba

Linglessou
Marinette Bois-Chèche
Ti Jean Pethro
Jean-Philippe Pethro
Grande Sobo
Adjinakou (the elephant mystère Agaou l'éphant)
Adahi Loko (Adan-hi Loco)
Kadia Bossou
Baron La Croix (The Cross)
Baron Cimetière (The Cemetery)
Baron Samedi (Saturday)
Grande Brigitte
Guédé Ti Wava
Guédé Ti Pété (Little-Break-wind)
Boli Shah (a family of loas)
Danbhalah Grand-Chemin (The Highway)
Mademoiselle Anaise
Mam'zelle Charlotte
Maîtresse Mam'bo
Marassah Guinin (African Twins)
Marassah Bois (Twins of the Wood)
Marassah Bord-de-Mer (Twins of the Seashore)
Erzulie Dos-bas (Low back)
Grande Allaba
Attiassou Yangodor
Similor
Guédé Z'eclairs (Lightning Bolts)
Guédé Nibbho
Guédé Vi
Loko Adan-he-co
Maître Ka-Fu (Legba, Master of the Crossroads)
Olishah
Ossou Gninmin
Grande Obatalah
Bayacou
Sim'bi d'l'eau (Simbi of the Water)
Ibo L'Asile
Ibo Can-Man
Maître Pem-bha

Dan Pethro
Sinigal
Ti Jean Pied-chèche (Dry Foot)
Ya Bô Fer
Simalo (the name which Antoine Simon, President of Haiti from
    1908 to 1911, gave his goat, which was a loa, following the
    tradition of divine right in the Dahomean monarchy)
Roi Louanges
Jean Zombi
Captain Zombi
Guédé Bon Poussière de la Croix (Good-Dust-of-the-Cross)
Bacossou
Guédé Doube
Guédé Fatras
Guédé Ti Clos
Guédé Docteur Piqures (Doctor Hypodermic)
Agu Roi Linsou
Danbhalah To Can
Amisi Wédo
Grande Miroi-Zé
Erzulie Boum'ba
Ogou Tonnerre (Baron Tonnerre—Thunder)
Bélécoun
Capalou Pem'ba
Brisé Pem'ba
Maloulou
Mavangou (a family of mystères)
Mitraille (Grapeshot)
Madame Travaux (Mrs. Works)
Sidor Pem'ba (Colonel Dan Pethro rite)
Fa-ou Dan-Tô
Ogou Baba (a general who is a retired trooper)
Mam'bo Ati-A-Sou
Guédé Souffrant (Suffering Guédé: Legba as Christ crucified)
Grand Bois Mégui
Adélaîde
Clairmésine Clairmeille
Ogou Balisère
Ibo Cossi

Mademoiselle Florida
Papa Houn'tò
Dame Houn'tò
Maître Cimetière (Master of the Cemetery)
Brutus Jean (Ti Brutus)
Général Jules Canmil
Guédé Ratalon (the first gravedigger)
Guédé Morpion (Guédé Ratalon's pick-man)
Captain Debas (an American mystère, also known as Deebat, or
     Debard)
Escalia Boum'ba
Trois Feuilles-Trois Racines (Three Leaves-Three Roots)
Marinette Pieds-Chèches (Dry Feet)
Ogou Dan Pethro
Cita
Zilah Moyo
Tiacou-Tiacou
Papa Pierre
Manman Diamant
Marie-Louise (a famous mystère of the War of Independence)
Ati-Danhi Ibo Loko (Accident Ibo Loko)
Trois Carrefours (Three Crossroads)
Jean-Pierre Pongoueh
Zo Flanco Pethro
Toro Pethro (Pethro Bull)
Quita (Kitha)
Kanga Pethro
Reine Congo Franc (Queen French Congo)
Six Milles Hommes (Six Thousand Men, probably Similor)
Dérazine
Djobolo Bossou
Séverine
Sarazine Jambé
Erzulie-Séverine-Belle-Femme (Beautiful Woman)
La Belle Vénus (The Fair Venus—Erzulie)
Ogou Palama
Grande Bossine
Grande Délaï
Dame Ténaîse

Dagoueh Bologoueh
Mouché Pierre
Ti Pierre (Little Peter)
Gros Pierre (Big Peter)
Sobo Quersou
Bazou
Nantiou
Zan-Madone

The Voodoo pantheon is far from complete in the preceding list. Scarcely one hundred pages would suffice to mention all the loas included in it, especially if all the etymological variants continually given the names of the loas by initiates were taken into account. For this reason many of the loas seem quite bizarre on account of their names, for example, *Ti Puce lan d'l'eau* (Little Flea-in-the-Water), *Mademoiselle Florida* (Miss Florida), *Fleurizon,* or *Grande Fleurizon* (Grandmother Fleurizon), and *Gédé Souffrant* (Suffering Guédé). These are variants of some of the great classical mystères. They assume these unusual names for their own occult reasons.

Classifying the Gods

The following is an attempt at a classification of the mystères according to the various rites or divisions of Voodoo, such as Rada and Pethro. This classification is necessarily arbitrary, owing to the fact that a mystère generally belongs to whatever rite he is "served" in, with the single exception of the so-called "Guinin" (African) mystères, who because of their traditional purity refuse to "work" in any but their own rites. The Guédés (the loas of death and of cemeteries) who have *noms vaillants* (names with the great mystères assume when they do not wish to appear under their real names) are classed separately, since it is difficult to assign them to particular rites because of the multiplicity of their names.

The Rada Mystères

Até Gbini Mon Sé
Yé Dan-Gbé
Danbhalah Wédo

Danbhalah Yé-Wé
Aida Wédo (Ayidahwédo)
Mawu-Lihsan
Lihsah
Legba Ati (n) Bon
Québiésou (Héviozo)
Grande Ai-Zan
Aizan Avélékéthé
Assatò
Adanmansih Wédo
Aganman, Caïman, Anolis
Adya Houn'tò
Agassou Allada
Maîtresse and Grande Erzulie
Fleurizon
Agoueh R Oyo
Agoueh Tha Oyo
Sim'bi Yandehzo
Sim'bi Yanphaca
Sim'bi Yanpolah
Marassah (Twins)
Avadra Bô-roi (Good King)
Loko Azamblo Guidi
Aroyo
Sobo
Badè
Badè-sih Cala Houn'sou
Houn'
Houn'sih
Houn'guénicon
Houn'gan
Houn'tò
Gougoune Dan Leh
Québiésou Dan Leh
La Sirène
La Baleine
An Oué-Zo
Silibo Vavo
Grande Vavo

Grande Sim'ba
A Dan-hi
Cousin Zaca
Zo
Zo Man Kilé
Sophie Badè
Agaou Comblé
Zinclizin
Azaca Médeh
Guédé Nouvavou
Guédé Mazaca
Zan Tha-hi
Zan Tha-hi Médeh
Ogou Bacouleh
Erzulie Fréda
Ti Pierre Dantor
Ti Jean
Bòcò Legba
Linglessou
Grande Sobo
Adanhi Loko
Baron La Croix (The Cross)
Baron Cimetiè (The Cemetery)
Baron Samedi (Saturday)
Grande Brigitte
Danbhalah Grand Chemin (The Highway)
Maîtresse Mam'bo
Marassah Guinin (African Twins)
Erzulie Dos-bas (Low Back)
Grande Allaba
Guédé Nibbho
Loco A Dan-hi-co
Maître Ka-Fu (Master of the Crossroads)
Bayacou
Sim'bi d'l'eau (Simbi of the Water)
Dan Pethro
Roi Louanges
Guédé Agu Roi Linsou
Danbhalah Tò Can

Amisi Wédo
Grande Miroi Zé
Bélécou-n
Grand Bois Mégui
Adélaïde
Clairmesine Clairmeille
Mademoiselle Florida
Papa Houn'tô
Dame Houn'tô
Captain Debas (the American mystère)
Papa Pierre
Manman Diamant
Marie-Louise
Ati Dan-hi Ibo Loko
Erzulie Séverine Belle-Femme (Fair Lady)
La Belle Vénus (Beautiful Venus)
Sobo Quersou

Mystères Belonging To All Rites

Assatò
Aganman, Caïman
Adya Houn'tò
Maîtresse et Grande Erzulie
Sim'bi d'l'eau
Sim'bi Yandehzo
Sim'bi Yanphaca
Sim'bi Yanpolah
Marassah
Houn'
Houn'sih
Houn'gan
Houn'guénicon
Houn'tò
Québiésou Dan Leh
Grande Sim'ba
Zo
Zo Man Kilé

Danbhalah Grand Chemin
Maîtresse Mam'bo (Grande Ai-Zan)
Maître Ka-Fu
Papa Houn'tò
Dame Houn'tò

The Rada-Dahomey Mystères

Até Gbini Mon Sé
Yé Dan Gbé
Ayidohwédo
Maou-Lihsah
Lihsan Gba Dya (Legba)
Legba Atin Bon (Adingban)
Québiésou
Ai-Zan
Sobo
Badè
An Qué Zo
Sophie Badé
Erzulie Fréda
Grande Sobo
Zan-Madone
A Dan-hi Loko
Erzulie La Belle Vénus

The Rada-Nago-Congo-Dahomey Mystères

La Sirène (Erzulie)
La Baleine (Erzulie)

The Nago Mystères

Ogou Fer (Dry Nago)
Ogou Bha Lin Dyo (Wet Nago)

Ogou Bha Tha Lah (Mixed Nago)
Ogou Chango (Nago, Pethro)
Adoum Guidi
Lem'ba Filé Sabre (Nago, Pethro)
Ogou Bha Da Gri
Ossangne
Ogou Yamsan (Nago, Pethro)
Ogou Cancannican (Nago Pethro)
Ogou Bhacouleh (Nago, Rada)
Ti Pierre Dantor (Nago, Rada, Dantor)
Ti Jean (Nago, Rada)
Bô-Sou Ashadeh (Nago, Dahomey)
Ashadeh Bòcò (Nago, Dahomey, Pethro)
Bolishah (Boli Shah)
Olishah (Oli Shah)
Grande O-Bhathalah
Bacossou
Ogou-Tonnerre (Nago, Pethro)
Ogou Baba
Ogou Balisère (Ogou Balisage)
Général Jules Canmil
Jean-Pierre Poungoueh
Ogou Palama

The Pethro Mystères

Ogou Chango (Pethro, Nago)
Sim'bi Y-An-Kitha
Lem'ba Filé Sabre (Pethro, Nago)
Ti Gougoune
Lem'ba Zaou (Pethro, Congo)
Zaou Pem'ba (Pethro, Congo)
Manman Pem'ba (Pethro, Congo)
Mackandal
Sim'ba Maza
Danbhalah La Flambeau (The Torch)
Linglinzin (Pethro, Rada)

Ogou Yamsan (Pethro, Nago)
Guédé Mazaca (Pethro, Rada)
Guédé L'Orage (The Storm)
Zazi Boulonnin (or Boulonmin)
Ogou Cancan Ni Can
Criminel Pethro
Prin'ga Maza (Pethro Maza)
Brisé Macaya
Brizé Pem'ba
Erzulie Toro (The Bull)
Erzulie Gé Rouge (Red-Eye)
Erzulie Mapian (Louse)
Ashadeh Bòcò (Pethro, Nago, Dahomey)
Bòcò Legba (Pethro, Rada)
Linglessou Bassin-sang (Pethro, Rada)
Marinette Bois-Chèche (Dry Wood)
Marinette Lumin-di-fé (Light-the-Fire)
Ti Jean Pethro
Jean-Philippe Pethro
Guédé Baron La Croix (Pethro, Rada)
Guéde Baron Cimetiè (Pethro, Rada)
Baron Samedi (Pethro, Rada)
Grande Brigitte (Pethro, Rada)
Similor
Guédé Nibbho (Pethro Rada)
Ibo Can-Man (Pethro, Ibo)
Maître Pem'ba (Pethro, Congo)
Dan Pethro
Ti Jean Pied Chèche (Dry Foot)
Simalo
Jean Zombi
Captain Zombi
Guédé Agu Roi Linsou (Pethro, Rada)
Ogou Tonnerre (Pethro, Nago)
Brisé Pem'ba (Pethro, Zandor)
Maloulou (Pethro, Congo)
Madame Travaux (Mrs. Works)
Sidor Pem'ba (Pethro, Congo)

Grand Bois Mégui (Pethro, Rada)
Escalié Boum'ba (Pethro, Boum'ba)
Trois Feuilles, Trois Racines (Three Leaves, Three Roots)
Marinette Pieds Chèches (Dry-Feet: Pethro, Zandor)
Ogou Dan Pethro (Nago, Pethro)
Marie Louise (Pethro, Rada)
Trois Carrefours (Three Crossroads)
Zo Flanco Pethro
Toro Pethro (The Bull)
Kanga Pethro
Six Milles Hommes (Six Thousand Men)
Djobolo Bossou (Pethro, Congo)

The Dantor Mystères

Ti Pierre Dan-Tor
Ti Jean Dan-Tor
Fa-ou Dan-Tor
Papa Pierre (Dantor, Rada, Nago)
Erzulie Dan-Tor

The Kitha Mystères

Ti Kitha Démembré
Quita

The Zandor Mystères

Brisé Pem'ba
Marisette Pieds Chèches (Dry-Feet)

The Ibo Mystères

Ibo Sou Aman
Ibo Kiki Lih Bô
Ibo L'Asile
Ibo Lélé
Ibo Can-Man (Ibo, Pethro)
Ibo Cossi (Ibo, Cossi)

The Congo Mystères

Sim'bi d'l'eau
Grande Alouba
Grande Aloumandia
Canga
Zin'ga
Lem'ba Za-ou (Congo, Pethro)
Man Inan
Madame Lah-Oué
Laoca (the Congo Legba)
Zaou Pem'ba (Congo, Pethro)
Manman Pem'ba (Congo, Pethro)
Roi Ou-Angole (Congo, Angola)
Marassah Congo Bord-de-Mer (Seashore)
Maître Pem'ba (Congo, Pethro)
Sinigal (Congo, Senegal)
Roi Louanges (Congo, Rada, Loango)
Caplaou Pem'ba
Maloulou (Congo, Pethro)
Sidor Pem'ba (Congo, Pethro)
Zilah Moyo
Reine Congo Franc
Djobolo (Congo, Pethro)
Bazou (Congo, Angola)

The Boum'ba Mystères

Cimetière Boum'ba (Boum'ba of the Cemetery)
Escalia Boum'ba

A Canga Mystère

Zoclimo

The Guedes

Guédé L'Orage
Guédé Cinq Jours Malheureux
Guédé Ti Puce Lan d'l'eau
Guédé Ti Wawa, or Ti Oua-Oué
Guédé Ti Pété
Guédé Vi (a child of the Guédés)
Guédé Bon Poussière de la Croix
Guédé Sabalah
Guédé Doube
Guédé Fatras
Guédé Ti Clos
Guédé Docteur Piqures
Guédé Souffrant
Guédé Ratalon
Guédé Morpion (Louse)

It may be observed that although most of the Guédés are listed separately, the most classic forms of Guédé are included among the Rada loas, for example, *Baron La Croix Guédé Nibbho (Nébo), Baron*

Cimetié, Guédé Mazaca, Baron Semedi, Guédé Nowvavou, Agu-Roi Lin-Sou, and *Guédé Houn'sou.*

As for the lesser Guédés, such as *Ti Pété* (Little Break-Wind), *Ratalon,* (Level-with-the-Heel, Laid-out, Prostrate), and *Ti Puce lan d'l'eau,* (Little-Flea-in-the-Water), their bizarre names derive from the caustic character of this race of loas. All the Guédés are pranksters.

The foregoing lists of mystères illustrate the difficulty previously mentioned with regard to placing any given mystère in any given rite, for the classification itself recognizes many mystères served in several rites—for example, the mystères which belong indifferently to all rites, and those who belong to the Rada-Dahomey-Nago-Congo group.

I have rejected any rigid classification of loas such as exists, for example, in strictly Haitian Voodoo, since their exclusively Pethro, Zandor, Congo, or Anmine character is subject to dispute; for, as a rule, a loa is "Zandor," or "Congo" simply because it is served in the Zandor or the Congo rite. This concept recalls the words of Sir James Frazer, who in his book *The Golden Bough,* Vol. I, page 165, denies the distinction between Janus and Jupiter which is suggested by certain writers on mythology: " . . . the names of the divinities being identical in substance, though varying in form with the dialect of the particular tribe which worshipped them. At first, when the peoples dwelt near each other, the difference between the deities would be hardly more than one of name; in other words, it would be almost purely dialectical. But the gradual dispersion of the tribes, and their consequent isolation from each other, would favor the growth of divergent modes of conceiving and worshipping the gods whom they had carried with them from their old home, so that in time discrepancies of myth and ritual would tend to spring up and thereby to convert a nominal into a real distinction between the divinities . . . thus it might come about that the same ancient deities, which their forefathers had worshipped together before the dispersion, would now be so disguised by the accumulated effect of dialectical and religious divergencies that their original identity might fail to be recognised, and they would take their places side by side as independent divinities . . . " Frazer is speaking of certain religious concepts found among Greek and Roman peoples. However, the same phenomenon is observed among African tribes. If by his transfer from Greece to Rome

Zeus became first *Jupiter Dianus*, then *Janus*, just so, *Héviozo*, migrating from the shores of Africa to the shores of Haiti has become *Québiésou Dan Leh.*

By the very fact that the social tradition is of ancestral origin like that of the Voodoo cult itself, it is a simple matter to discover in the pantheon of the loas a governmental form of the social hierarchy. For example:

Legba Adingban ... King of kings
Aïda Wédo .... Queen of heaven, earth, and angels
Ogou Ferraille ..... General
Azaca Médé .... Minister of the Interior and of Agriculture

All of these important loas are representatives of a power deriving from an occult origin, a power in fact controlled by the mystère Legba. Their power is regarded as passing, by means of Voodoo magic, from mere potentiality to useful action. Functionally, they are all under the houn'gan's control who, in point of hierarchy, is their chief. The houn'gan, then, controls a force which, on the human-principal level of Legba, synthetizes all the powers of the loas. Therefore he is the one who, in the course of Voodoo ceremonies, is chiefly responsible for moving from the potentiality to the magical act.

The Roles of the Gods

For the purpose of clarifying the roles of all the mystères, it will suffice to present several traditional interpretations of the important fundamental loas of the Voodoo Cult. These roles show the reasons why the Haitian Voodooist considers the gods vitally inseparable from himself.

Silibo Vavou, or
Schibhlo Vavau

Erzulie adorning herself;
science; omniscience; prescience:
the holy spirit of initiation.

Marassah

The sun as magic regency of the
sky through birth and rebirth.

Danbhalah

The return of animal or *bossale*

	(uninitiated) matter to the sun through initiation.
Ogou Fer	Logic; reason; wisdom; philosophy; armed and intelligent intercession.
Can-zo	The power which directs the raw or *bossale* matter towards the solar regions.
The Rada Mystères	The loas of intelligence.
Sim'bi Y-An-Pha-Ca	The cosmic culture.
The Nago Oyo Mystères	The voluntary and conscious reflection of initiated matter in the high atmosphere of the celestial constellations through Erzulie; that is, by the principle of the Virgin taken as the "magic mirror" (Agoueh Tha Oyo).
Agoueh R Oyo	The will to be reflected magically in the ritual waters (Agoueh Tha Oyo) or in the abyss represented by the socle of the center-post.
Guédé Houn'sou	The ground of the oum'phor and the asson; the Virgin and Child; the moon and the sun.
Québiésou Dan Leh	Supreme justice, or the thunderstone of the bagui; the religious morality of the oum'phor.
Baya-cou, or Bha Ya Chou } Yé-ch-ou	Cosmic work of the day and the night (Je-sus).
Bha-ca, or Ba-Ka	The science of talismans, or telesmatic Voodoo, representing magically the two cosmic priesthoods:

BHA = Orient   KA = Occident
          Sun   Moon
          Man   Woman
        (Legba)   (Erzulie)

The Mavangou Mystères

Houn'gan

Houn'guénicon

Oum'phor

Legba (Master of the Cross-
        roads)

Africa

Ati-Dan I-Bo Loko

The loas of necromancy.

The guardian of the magic powers
of the sun.

The ritual prayer and its cabalistic effect; stellar mercy.

The Holy City; Jerusalem; the
Zodiac; the twelve cabalistic
abodes of Erzulie; the gates of
Zion; the secrets of the astral
light.

Geometric separation of the cabalistic matter represented by
the ritual water, which produces the magic possibilities of
the visible phenomenon; practical consolidation or central-
ization of the dispersed powers
of astral space; geocentric util-
ization of the stellar atmosphere.

The galaxy which governs the
holy spirit; the geometric and
spiritist system of the sun, represented by the mystère Legba
Ati-Bon Ati-Dan I-bo Lo-ko.

The tree-principle; the tree of
good and evil; the center-post
of the peristyle.

Guédé Ni-Bo, or Râ Nibbho   The risen Christ; the rising sun;
                              the vertical line of the center-
                              post; the oriental Voodoo priest-
                              hood.

These orthodox interpretations reveal that despite all deformations
of the magic formulas of origin, the causes of which are due to the
particular psychology of certain sects and tribes, Voodoo is nevertheless based upon the great supernatural loas whose duty is to bring
the material body back into the higher atmospheres through initiation
and ritual.

These symbolic identifications have such value as to predominate
universally among Voodooists. It is therefore useless to attempt to
separate the Congo mystères from the Anmine, the Anmine from the
Pethro, or the Rada from the Nago. Between these "rites" or "nations
of loas," all that matters is the difference in the manner of applying
the science of magic; for nothing of a scientific nature can exist apart
from these great basic loas. Thus, the "nations of Africa" (because
Africa conceals the galaxy which governs the Holy Spirit) have, each
of them, a hidden significance which, in the Voodoo frame of reference, is a scientific universality that differs from tribe to tribe. However, from the purely "national-scientific" or "tribal-scientific" level
to the purely aesthetic and moral level, the differences between the
rites are confirmed. For example, the Rada rite is, as a rule, more
moral than the Pethro, since the Rada is traditionally the rite par excellence that governs the moral aspects of the sky under the form of
the mystère *Ai-Zan A Vélé-Kétheh*. The mystères *Ai-Da* Wé-do and
Da-nbhalah Wé-Do are the visible manifestations of Ra-Da, the serpent, in the oum'phor.

The ethical differences in the ruling position of the serpent *Da-n*
are therefore placed in relation to the basic rites of Voodoo thus:

RADA .... The Star, or Upper Air
NAGO .... Metal
CONGO .... Water
PETHRO .... Fire
IBO .... The Word
MINE, OR AN-MINE ..... The Earth

However, each rite, having inherited the tradition in its entirety, is in itself a complete magic system of such a kind that it contains the entire body of symbolic significations. The only difference is that each rite reveals to its own initiates, by its own system of symbolism, its own individual character and the individual cosmic temperament of the African "nation" with which it is identified.

Danbhalah - - - the Serpent God

The snake vertebras that adorn the assons of houn'gans and mam'bos represent Danbhalah, while the cephalo-rachidian axis, as well as the fertilizing seed which makes Legba a phallic mystère, are represented by the center-post of the peristyle. Da, in magic, represents the oldest of the ancestors, a fact that gives him the right to have the "cosmic egg" as his ritual nutriment. Because of his very great age—the age of humanity—tradition holds that Danbhalah Houé-Do never speaks. He expresses himself, rather, by the hissing of a snake—the sound produced by those whom he possesses during ceremonies. In the Pethro rite, the ritual whistle represents this snake-hissing. Since Pethro is the rite of solar fire (hwé-zo), the hissing is heard in the roar of the flames.

Voodoo langage—the words used in chants—originated from the hissing of the snake, and is, in fact, the direct expression of what is highest placed in the astral-causal. In the Voodoo tradition, then, Danbhalah corresponds to the asson and the bell with which the houn'gan, the highest member of the hierarchy, officiates. The official attributes of the houn'gan correspond to the rattlesnake, otherwise known as the couleuvre-à-clochette (bell-snake). This musical serpent is therefore the most significant expression of the musical "wood" and the musical calabashes of the joukoujou, of the calabash and the wooden handle of the asson, as well as of the circle and the serpent-adorned wood of the center-post.

Since the center-post is, accordingly, a "solar expression," all the sacred music of Voodoo produced by the batteries of Pethro, Rada, Congo, and Ibo drums is likewise a solar expression. The center-post of the peristyle is therefore the "magic support" of Voodoo through the mystère Legba Ati Bon.

Since the "reptilian line of the wood" descends from the astral to possess its "white horses" with the personality of Danbhalah, this mystère appears always to "swim" in grace and to delight totally in metaphysical and hyperphysical pleasure while seeming at the same time to be lost in active and contemplative joy. This phenomenon is due to the three types of beatitudes recognized in theology: the active, the contemplative, and the joyful.

Now the serpent of the oum'phor personifies the total number of beatitudes which the initiates double to fourteen: seven for the body as corporal qualities, seven for the soul as spiritual virtues. So also are all the other mystères to be considered as so many serpents; and while the serpent Danbhalah or Dan-Gbé expresses the geometric perfection of which all the loas and all ritual performance partake, the loas are all serpents more or less perfect, according to the degree of knowledge they possess.

Danbhalah expresses geometric perfection because in his quality as a mystère he corresponds to the gifts of the holy spirit through his beatitudes, for the church's doctors of theology recognize that the beatitudes correspond to the seven gifts of the holy spirit. Danbhalah is therefore aptly named Dan-(Gift)Bhalah Wé-Do. Hence, his geometric expression is total and perfect, because, as in theology, a beatitude is, according to St. Thomas, an "operation and ultimate perfection," while Aristotle has defined it as being contained in "the most perfect operation by reason of its power, its practice, and its object." The ritual attitudes of Danbhalah recall to the minds of initiates the best definition of the word "beautitude" that theology has to offer for the instruction of the uninitiated, namely "the ultimate end of rational nature."

The Voodoo Virgin

The female energy of Legba is Erzulie, the Virgin of the Voodoo initiates, commonly called Maîtresse Erzulie. She personifies another species of serpent, short and coiled upon itself, which feeds upon bananas and which lives chiefly in the water. Etymologically this short, quick-moving serpent which is thought to run over the virgin ground like a bolt of celestial fire, derives from *érinos*, which means "fig tree" or "banana tree;" and from *Erigone*, the constellation of the Virgin. Consequently, Erzulie is the most attractive mystère of Voodoo. She is precisely the Voodoo heart, which she shares with Legba, and which is also his attribute. Magically, Erzulie is the lover of Legba in the same sense that Erigone is the lover of Bacchus, that is to say, as mistress of the water she is the ritual water, while Legba is the eucharistic wine.

In the Voodoo tradition, Maîtresse Erzulie fulfills several roles. She is the mystère of eloquence—the mystère of the word, which she shares as an attribute along with Legba. She is the mystère of jealousy, vengeance, and discord, and on the other hand, the mystère of love, perpetual help, good will, health, beauty, and fortune. Thus, under the same name of *Eris*, or *Eros*, she possesses the "golden apple" which in Greek mythology, is the equivalent of the *figue-banane* of the magical tradition of Voodoo. It is this *pomme-banane* (apple-banana) that she casts among the Three Graces as the mystère of discord, and which she reaps eventually and shrewdly as mystère of beauty and of sacred music under the name of Venus. The tradition then shows her exercising her supernatural powers by means of two serpents that she employs as a magic weapon, at once contradictory and harmonious, brandishing one in each hand, and binding in mysterious fashion in her hair.

The Erzulies of vengeance and of ugliness are the terrible loas that bear the names of Marinette-Bois Chèche, Erzulie Toho, Erzulie Zandor, Erzulie Mapiangueh. These mystères twist in fantastic convulsions, indicating even saturnalian cannibalism. They "walk" on the "point" *z'araignée* (spider).

The Erzulies of wealth and beauty are the great virgins of Voodoo—Tsilah Wédo and Aida Wédo (the serpent-woman of Danbhalah Wédo), who are the two classic wives of Legba. They "walk" on the points of the fruitful earth, of the "sweet and ripe banana," of fidelity, of peace, of pure milk, and of the heart.

The tragic Erzulies of jealousy worship fire. These are the ones who fought in the ranks with the soldiers of the war for the independence of Haiti against Napoleon's armies as artillerymen and as prostitutes who instructed the insurgent slaves. They are fond of alcohol mixed with pepper, raw rum (tafia) mixed with gunpowder, and their magic attribute is the heart pierced and bloodied with the dagger of the Ogous.

The pure Erzulies of fidelity and of the fecund earth have as a magic attribute a vèvè of a heart surmounted by a stellar emblem. This heart is decorated with the horns of the Ram of the Golden Fleece which the ritual of the *loa-blancs* (white loas) offers to Agoueh R Oyo, the marine spouse of Erzulie. The heart is marked off in squares to reveal the peace which reigns on the earth when the virtues of the Virgin prevail through her bidding. The points placed in the middle of the squares indicate that this bidding is the solar achievement of the post which is right in the middle of the heart and which, like the center-post, corresponds exactly with the banana tree whose leaves lead to Ifé under the name *bateau d'Erzulie* (bark of Erzulie). This heart is that of the central mystère which Voodoo initiates call "The Queen of Heaven and Earth." Erzulie, as bark or as wife of Agoueh, corresponds to the bed of banana leaves which leads the initiates to the sky.

Following are several names used to call Erzulie in the course of a service: Maîtresse Erzulie Fréda Dahoumin, Négresse Imamou Ladeh, Négresse To-Can, Négresse Miroi-Zé, Négresse Za-Gaza, Négresse Rada Fréda Dahoumin, Lorvana Fréda-sih Fré-Da, Lih Fréda-sih, Lih Fré-Da et l'Fréda li Dahounin d'accord, Négresse Fla-voudoun Fréda, Négresse Ci-za-fleur voudoun, Négresse Ci-bracan, Négresse Thabor Mangnan Voudé.

Other Voodoo Gods

Ogou Bhathalah is a part of the army of Ogou loas considered in the African tradition as the fathers of alchemy. In the universal tradition, Bhathalah corresponds to the first large blade of the Tarot (the Juggler), whose hat is the sign of the "universal life." This is the *Magus* (Wise One) or spirit par excellence. Bhathalah personifies the "discipline of chaos" because it is he who directs, with the magic wand, the cosmic traffic. Bhathalah "disentangles the roads" by placing himself, like a traffic officer, at the magic crossroads. The scriptural reference to his occult function is found in Ezekiel XXI, 19-21: "The Lord says, Appoint thee two ways, that the sword of the king of Babylon may

come . . . For the king of Babylon stood at the parting of the way, at
the head of the two ways, to use divination." The "swordstroke of Ogou" means that the Ogou mystères (loas of
fire) or "stellar powers, creators of the intellect" are descended from
heaven through a fissure shaped like the female sex organ represented
by the planet Venus (Erzulie, in Voodoo). These are the mystères who
are "forgers," like the *aelohim* which descend from the Jewish *Aziluth*,
or like the "Lords of the Flame" in Indian mythology. The Ogous in
the Voodoo tradition bear the "fire of heaven" or the "luminous fire of
Venus" shaped in the forge to represent a short serpent which traverses
the planetary earth and sows fire. "Ogou's swordstroke" means also the
act of kissing the top of the flagpoles during the course of the ritual
Voodoo salutations performed by the flagbearers.

In Voodoo, *Luci-Fer*, whose name is also Ogou-Fer, is Venus, the
morning star. It is called "Bayacou star" because it accompanies the
sun each morning to explain the "earthly necessities" or "needs."

Mademoiselle Charlotte is a loa who manifests herself with the personality traits of a white woman. She is therefore regarded as a European or Caucasian loa who "works" in the Voodoo pantheon. However,
she appears during the course of Voodoo ceremonies only rarely,
possibly because of her non-African origin.

An extremely fastidious spirit, Mademoiselle Charlotte loves the
strict observance in her honor of all the niceties of ritual protocol. She
prefers to speak French; so it is extremely curious to hear her speak
at a Voodoo ceremony, especially since her "horse" is invariably a
black Haitian. It is nothing less than astonishing to hear an unedu-
cated peasant, whose ignorance of French is beyond question, suddenly handle the language so perfectly. Whenever Charlotte appears,
she astonishes people as much as certain mystères who enable their
"mounts" to speak fluent Spanish or English.

She is "served" in much the same way as Maîtresse Erzulie. She
enjoys sweet rose-tinted, blue-, white-, or cream-colored beverages;
water sweetened with syrup; all kinds of non-alcoholic liqueurs; although she never refuses a good drink of clairin, a fact that suggests
she "walks" not only in the Rada rite but sometimes in the Péthro rite
as well. Her favorite color is rose. She is passionately fond of *acassan*,
a delicious, mushy drink consisting of boiled cornmeal sweetened with
cane juice of the kind Haitians call *gros sirop batterie*. This juice, how-

ever, must be exceedingly clear and highly refined; otherwise she will replace it with plain white sugar. She prefers the meat of young chickens as her ritual food offering, but the meat must be extremely tender.

Mademoiselle Charlotte is a *voudoun* whose services are difficult to obtain. She refuses to "work" for just anyone at all, but only for people to whom she takes a fancy.

Dinclinsin is another European mystère. Legend has it that both Dinclinsin and Mademoiselle Charlotte came to Haiti with the colonists. Once the cult had become established on Haitian soil, he began to appear in the Voodoo ceremonies of the African slaves in the same way as the other mystères, by "possessing" a ritual "horse."

Dinclinsin became a loa of the Rada rite. He is greatly feared because of his extreme severity. He apparently also "walks," like Charlotte, in the Péthro rite as well, since he is not averse to rum, tafia, or clairin. However, he does not drink, but rather pours the liquor into his pockets. His special trick is to pour the liquor into his pockets without getting his clothes wet. The liquor does not remain in his pockets, nor does it trickle out! No one can see where it goes! (Certain other mystères drink through the nose, the ears, and even the eyes. One mystère, *Pin'ga*, even eats razor blades.)

4

Symbols of Voodoo

VOODOO has many important symbols to aid its magic. Only through the use of these symbols is the Voodoo adherent able to attain the assistance of the loas in helping him with his earthly problems.

The Vèvès

The *vèvès* are without any doubt the most spectacular ceremonial factor of Voodoo. The vèvès are designs traced upon the ground of the peristyle or the oum'phor, or upon all sorts of objects, even ritual food. In the region of Port-au-Prince the vèvès are made with great care so that they are clearly visible and almost geometrically flawless. Elsewhere, however, it is made carelessly and crudely; and in some regions it is not used at all, for example in the oum'phors in the neighborhood of Gonaives.

The *vèvès* represent *figures of the astral forces* in a different way than the asson does. Their manufacture in the oum'phor is the reproduction by Voodoo magic of the astral forces themselves. This fact signifies that the vèvès, considered as astral forces, are necessarily personified by the star-ancestors whose cult is Voodoo—these ancestors being themselves personified by the loas, the spirits, the voudoun, or the mystères that "mount" the Voodooists.

In the course of Voodoo ceremonies, the reproduction of the astral forces represented by the vèvès obliges the loas (who are representations of heavenly bodies, stars, and planets) to descend to earth. On first consideration, this may appear improbable; however, nothing is truer, more obvious, or more palpable, and the explanation, given here for the first time, can be easily verified. As a visitor at a Voodoo service, one has only to consider the interrelation of the ritual factors as explained here in order to be easily convinced.

Depending upon the rite, the vèvè is traced with wheat flour, corn meal, Guinea-flour (wood ashes), powdered leaves, red brick powder, rice powder (face powder), and even gunpowder, powdered charcoal, bark, or roots.

As a rule, the milder rites such as the Rada, a solar rite, require white or yellow wheat. Tradition, though not always respected, demands that corn meal be used for the intermediate or less mild rites, whereas red brick powder or red dust or ashes belong to the *fire rites* whose cabalistic agents can, if need be, serve upon the *points-chauds* (hot-points)—not that these rites are fundamentally or necessarily evil, but rather because they have a greater tendency to burn when they are improperly or imprudently employed.

The powder of leaves, if the leaves are of the soothing variety, can be used for the mystères of the *points-frettes* (cold-points). If the powder is made of noxious leaves or merely of the "stinging" variety, it can "walk with" the so-called "Bois-Piquant" (pungent-wood) loas, the loas of the fiery rites: the *Pethro* and the *Zandor*.

Gunpowder serves to precipitate magically the mystères.

Face powder, scarcely used in Haiti, if at all, for vèvès, is traditionally employed for the brilliant mystères that "walk on the resplendent points" of the Sun: *Erzulie Za-Gaza*, the mystère *Joltière Viscière*, and *Legba Brillant Soleil*. For face powder symbolizes the purification, at a very high degree, of the ceremonial and sacrificial material. These brilliant mystères correspond necessarily to the most splendid stellar and planetary elements in the whole Voodoo organization of Legba Ati-Bon, not only because the magic system of Legba *is* the solar system, but also because the formula which designates the various types of powder is a part of Legba's own name: *ati-n*. *Ati-n*, then, means *ati-* ("magic wood" or "magic master") and *-n* ("of astral space").

Therefore, in considering this vèvè which is a synthesis of space, of the astral, and of their powers through Legba, we see a synthesis of the vèvè principle.

In the ritual geometry of Voodoo, most of the vèvès include the serpent as a symbol of the transmigration of souls, since God, or the serpent *Da*, in accordance with the Platonic tradition, is primarily a geometrician.

In principle, the Voodoo vèvès are three astral planes that are the three *"pneumes"* of the African Cabala, being the three stages of the alchemic *"souffleurs"* or *"prompters."* These three astral planes are arranged in the diagram according to the magical attributes of the loas. This is the meaning given these planes by the tradition of the Great Solar Invisibles of Voodoo: (1) the invisible source of the stars, or the divine cosmos of omniscience, represented by the father or *"Plerome,"* which is the idea of the preexisting light of the sun; (2) the visible stars whose light, coming from the Plerome is filtered by the moon or planetary cosmos of science, represented by the son or *"Paraclete"* which is the light of the sun; (3) the tangible objects, or physical cosmos of omnipotence of omniscience, represented by the mother as incarnate mystères (the loa "crisis") or *"Ophanim."*

In Voodoo, the father is "Omnipotent" or *"Até-Gbi-Ni-M-On-Sé,* as "Inexpressible" (the fire-air serpent); the son is the "Knowing One" or *"Lé-Gba Ati-Gbon,* as "Expression of the Inexpressible Invisible" (snake-wood); the mother is the "Omniscient" or *Ai-Da Hwé-Do,* as "Concretion of the Inexpressible Grand Invisible" (earth-eater serpent).

The three astral planes correspond to a serpent-synthesis which is *ophitomorphic* or *ophitopentamorphic,* that is to say, which unites to-gether as a macrocosm, all the elements of the microcosm or "human being." Thus it is that as serpent (*ophi-*) and mystère (*os* or *so*) with five heads (pentamorphic) these planes correspond to the five degrees of the Loa:

SOD	Mystères or Loas
THO-RAH	Letter (of the Loa)
MI-CH-NA-as	Spirit (of the Loa)
THA-EL-MUD	Ritual (of the Loa)
GUE-MA-RAH	Complement (of the Loa)

These are the universal similarities of what Voodoo calls vèvès: the
Ky-il-k-or, which like the vèvè is a ritual diagram designed ceremonially by the Tibetans on the ground with colored powders; the Man-Da-
Lah of the Hindus; the Persian, Arabian, Berber Tha-pi or Tapis, upon
which the faithful squats or kneels in order to arise towards the Invisibles; the magic buckler of the Aztecs and Toltecs; the Ora-i-Bi
Po-Wa-Nu of the Precolumbian Indian rituals; the Chinese Lit or Lih;
and the sand paintings of the American Indians. The vèvè, like its
parallels, is a geometric, propitiatory support of planetary origin, and
at the same time a condenser of astral forces designed to lead on the
sacrificial victims.

Every time the celebrant prepares to trace a vèvè he should say,
after orienting the material to be used in making the diagram, "By the
power of the Loa LETE-MAGIE, Nègre Danhomé, all the vèvès,
Nègre Bhacoulou Thi-Kaka."

The Assen

The assen is another synthesis in Voodoo, a greater one, it might be
said, than the vèvè. It is an iron object, a rod surmounted by a round
plate fastened horizontally, which from a hermetic standpoint relates
to the loas of fire and the forge who, beginning with the siderial action
of the heavenly bodies, are at the base of Voodoo doctrine and revelation. Thus, although the vèvès by geometric sympathy attract the
astral powers of the loas, in order to oblige them to "work" in the
peristyle or in the oum'phor or anywhere else, the power of the assen,
if it has been prepared well, is stronger, in the sense that it is more
compact and more concentrated. By its magical principle which is the
finest and the most highly developed, it serves, as a ritual object, to
make an unfailing success of any intercession in the form of a prayer
or a sacrificial offering. For this reason govis and candles are placed
upon the assen, the ritual form of which may be anything from that
of a stake or a simple cross to the most complex shapes, more complex,
in fact, than the cabalistic form of the parasol.

Placed upon the assen, the govis and candles have a remarkable
power of intercession. Consequently, every sacrificial offering presented in proper fashion upon the small iron plate atop the assen has

a much greater chance of being accepted by the mystères for whom it is intended.

In Africa, at any rate in Dahomey, from the moment a person is initiated into Voodoo, he automatically acquires his assen. There are even regular markets specializing in the sale of assens.

Amulets and Talismans

Amulets and talismans, called *ouangas* and *bakas*, represent a sort of superior soul to the Voodoo adherent. The baka plays the role of guardian angel, while the ouanga fulfills the function attributed to an image, a scapular, a rosary, or a chaplet. The Voodooist usually carries such a talisman and may address it any time external danger threatens him.

The baka represents two forces: a superior force or aerial soul, and an inferior force or terrestrial soul. The fusion of these elements lends a rather dangerous character to this magic entity which is the perfect baka. A person has only to serve the baka incorrectly to have it turn against its owner and do him irremediable harm by reason of the very, duality of its composition. On the other hand, whoever knows how to serev the baka obtains amazing results from it.

In Haiti, the term *baka* has come to have a somewhat pejorative meaning, most likely because bakas have sometimes been employed for doubtful purposes. Whoever possesses a baka has at his disposal an evil power as well as a beneficial power. The evil power overcomes the beneficial (as with all other powers) if the owner of the baka fulfills his destiny under the influence of the evil power. However, if it is the beneficial power that he "serves," then the baka is simply beneficial.

All things considered, an account of the analysis and a description of all the various Voodoo-prepared ouangas can be omitted because, considered from the standpoint of magic, they may be included with all such magical preparations as bakas, which have in essence and purpose the nature of the two souls—the superior and the inferior.

The Voodoo baka, for the person knowing how to prepare or employ one, represents all the legions of angels and demons over which King Solomon had power, according to Voodoo tradition. Solomon was the

perfect initiate, the representative of the "temple." Thus, because
he had in his possession a magic figure which embraced all esoteric
signs, he made use of both angels and demons as he desired. The sign,
which may not be revealed to the uninitiated, has reference to Christ
(the Voodoo Legba) as "Master of the Invisibles," and its magic correspondence is the sun.

The Voodooist does not exaggerate, then, when he claims that for
himself alone the baka synthetizes the entire ritual and religious constitution and all the magic practice of Voodoo. All the mystères are
found in its clever composition. It is simultaneously a magic charm,
protection, sacrifice, and performance; a terrestrial soul, a celestial
soul, a cult, atheism, a magic weapon, threat, and danger, a magic
prohibition, sacrificial victim; the concept of divinity, demonism,
riches, catastrophe, health, sickness, life and death.

The Voodoo baka has an importance in magic of such a kind that
every great initiate in the cult realizes that it may perfectly represent
all possible and imaginable practices of the cult as well as of Voodoo
magic. However, it would be wrong to believe that the baka principle,
in magic as in religion, is limited to Voodoo alone. Persistent research
reveals it everywhere, though under different names. In the learned
magic of the Egyptian temples Osiris, as the mystère who guides the
souls of the dead, personifies it, playing the same part that Ra Nibbho
plays in Voodoo magic, since in Egypt the baka has a double function
which, for those who understand its employment, is not one of disagreement or occult discord, but rather of harmony, happy union,
practical coalescence, and success in magic.

Baka, in the magic of Egypt just as in the magic of Haiti, has the
following meaning, understood even by the uninitiated: the mystère
ba or *bha*—found for example in the name of the mystère Dan-Bha-Lah
Wé-Do and of the Nago mystère Ba-cossou—is the superior soul which
resides in the material body from its embryonic stage only to inculcate
in it the idea of the good. At death it returns to the high solar regions
of the atmosphere where the Voodoo cult has its magical origin, letting
the dead and decaying body remain with the inferior soul with which
it had shared the body during life.

The inferior soul is then the *ka*, or *ca*. Hence, after death the body
is said to be *ka-ba*. The *ka* does not rise to the high atmospheric regions of the sun at the death of the body. It remains, by its nature,
with the corpse, hovering about and battening on its noxious stench

as if the earth which contains the decay of the putrifying flesh were its own psyche. It even abides in all the objects that once belonged to the corpse, and it is responsible for all the dread that the deceased's close friends experience in the houses in which he lived. Certain magical operations confer upon it a terrible power. Some houn'gans go and gather up the *ka* in the cemetery, where it naturally stays hovering over and feeding upon the corpse. These houn'gans then make use of it in "sending a 'mort' (dead person)" to take possession of, for example, an enemy, and a special magical operation is required in order to "remove the 'mort' from the body" of the individual whom the *ka* has possessed.

And so, whenever a person brings flowers to place upon a tomb, or "gives a feast" to the dead, it is the *ka* that, consciously or unconsciously, he is symbolically and magically assuaging. A kind prayer, a pretty flower, sweet music, mitigates its pernicious instincts and restores it to the less abyssal regions of the tomb. But the greatest blessing one can bestow upon the *ka* consists in magically purifying it to the extent of elevating it to the high region of the *ba*. Special sacrifices in the Voodoo rites lead to this elevation, and this type of sacrifice comes under the designation of *"boulez zain les morts"* or *"ouanzain."*

In the so-called "froid" (cold) rites, the *ka's* deliverance is brought about by the *cassez-canari* ceremony, which consists, substantially, in breaking one or more *canaris* (jars) with blows of a stick, and then depositing the broken pieces at a crossroads or at some other designated spot. This operation is accompanied by funereal music called *"bô-houn,"* produced by beating upon calabashes held over the surface of water.

The Joukoujou

The notched and graduated pole called the *joukoujou* represents the Tree of Good and Evil—the *arbre-sec* ("dry tree" or Sun) and the *arbre-mouillé* ("wet tree" or Moon). Because of its double-faced magic, it "walks" both in the Pethro and in the Rada rites, the two "polar rites" of Voodoo.

The joukoujou, in the powers of the astral, consequently represents the Balance which cabalistically serves to weigh out both good and evil. On the one hand the Guédé loas personify death; on the other hand the Legba loas personify life. For this reason the *joukoujou* is the traditional symbol of the ensemble of loas.

The pole of Guédé is called "wet," since Guédé is the mystère of the physical fertility which he exemplifies in his behaviour during a ceremony. When Legba uses the pole as his staff, however, it is called "dry," because Legba is the loa of virginal fertility. The two loas together represent, therefore, the two extreme poles of cosmic and cabalistic eroticism. Like the handle of the asson, the wooden pole of the joukoujou, through its similar symbolism to the center-post, is one of the principal elements of Voodoo. Both of these instruments are, in fact, images or doublings of the center-post.

The lower part of the *joukoujou* is called the "black horse" or "black dog," (meaning the opposite of life). The upper part is called the "white horse" or "white dog;" wherefore the Guédé loas dress in black when they possess someone, while Danbhalah's ritual horses put on white. Consequently, the lower part of the pole refers to the Guédés' domain of death, and the upper part to the Legbas' domain of life. The black horse or black dog is "mounted," in principle, by the chief mystère of the cemetery: Baron Samedi, the astral Saturn. The white horse or white dog, on the other hand, is "mounted" by the mystère Danbhalah, the astral source of the sun. Hence, in principle, Danbhalah's traditional dress during possessions is white, while the Guédés show a marked preference for black or at least very dark clothing. The extreme difference in taste of these two groups of mystères shows that the pole of the joukoujou, in its geometric totality, represents by its notches all stages of Voodoo initiation from that of the houn'sih bossales to that of the houn'gan.

The Balance, which in the Astral is the major symbol of the joukoujou, "walks" on the cabalistic points of the calabash that ascends and descends on the notched pole, that is to say, on all the magic points of Erzulie Fréda Dahomé Tocan Miroisé Zagaza, the Magic Mirror. This mirror-pole, marked off in degrees or notches, belongs to Legba and Baron Cemetery (another name for Baron Samedi), and is the same pole that is found in the hands of the Egyptian Thoth or the Greek Hermes. It weighs the qualities that permit the physical body to have a soul matching a particular degree of initiation, the metempsychosis of Guédé being considered as a test of initiation. For this reason the djévos (initiation chambers) of ancient oum'phors were themselves considered as tombs. In the story of Moses' initiation at the hands of Pethro, it is reported that Moses was actually dead during the entire period of his initiatory trial when he was confined in the *djévo*, just as the Voodoo initiates are confined today. Now just as every "degree" of the soul corresponds, in magic, to a "degree" of color, the notches on the joukoujou correspond to the various colors on the center-post of Legba (who stands for the life which successively follows each separate death according to degrees), and these colors in turn not only match the rainbow of Erzulie (upon the "point" of Ai-Da Houé-Do, the principal wife of Legba) but they also assume the reptilian form of Danbhalah Houé-Do.

Perfumes

If the *assen* represents one of the best means of transmitting sacrificial offerings from the earth to the most highly evolved loas of the astral, *perfumes* likewise hold a high place among ritual factors. The perfumes are not employed in the rites without purpose, or simply for vanity's sake, to enhance mortal individuals; rather, they are used in the service of the immortals, who are the loas that mortals serve in the ritual. Perfume may even be applied to all the other components of the ritual, in which they play a pre-eminent part.

It will be recalled that the mystère Erzulie has, as her metaphysical attribute, everything that pertains to self-adornment and personal hygiene, such as toilet water, soap, plain water, comb, brush, pins, and brooches. The most prominent of these items are her greates magical attributes: brooches, dresses, kerchiefs, negligees, silks, lace, embroidery, foulards, and above all, jewelry.

Consequently, since the mystère Maitresse Erzulie personifies the *Ceremonial and Sacrificial Material which ascends*, everything pertaining to self-adornment that is composed of the finest material occupies, in magic, a transcendent place. It follows naturally and by analogy that perfumes hold first place in the magic of transcendence. Furthermore, the finest gift that a person can give a loa is a bottle of perfume, or even a drop of perfume. Given perfume, a mystère is immediately *ravished*, his immateriality being allowed, as it were, a sort of *super-immaterility*.

Perfume offered is more efficacious if it is the kind that the loa to whom it is offered prefers. Every mystère has his own particular perfume, inasmuch as this perfume has its counterpart in what the Voodoo Initiatic calls the *Sacred Osmology*, or *Science of Odors*.

Just as every mystère is identified with a degree in the astral atmosphere, every perfume has there its counterpart attaching to its mystère. Consequently, one very often sees the houn'gan sprinkling the *astral atmosphere* of the oum'phor with perfume. Unfortunately, Haitian houn'gans have gotten into the habit of choosing Florida Water as the ritual perfume. This choice is apparently based upon economic considerations (Florida Water is relatively inexpensive), rather than upon the established preference of the mystères themselves. Perhaps the name of this perfume has something to do with the choice: one of the mystical forms of Erzulie is a mystère called *Florizon*, or *Fleurison!*

The leaves that enter into the composition of the magic baths, as well as all other ingredients employed in the magic of the peristyles and of the oum'phors proper, are chosen primarily because of their odors; for the material itself of any object has no cabalistic significance at all, just as if it were entirely bereft of soul or power without its scent.

Ritual Flags

The magnificent ritual flags are made right in the oum'phor. They are fashioned of colored cloth corresponding to the chromatic temperaments of the mystères under whose influence they are made, and all their beauty lies in the designs which artists, themselves initiates, first create, then embellish with multicolored pailettes. A flag consecrated, for example, to Ogou Fer would be adorned with a pailette design in the colors of the mystère representing Saint James on his white horse battling the infidels.

The ritual flags demonstrate the importance in magic of the acceptance of ceremonial offerings by the mystères to whom the offerings are dedicated. They symbolize this very acceptance which is referred to as "the ravishing of the sacrificial material by the Invisibles." Furthermore they symbolize the material already accepted, already "ravished," in the highest atmospheres of the Astral Light by the "wind of the spirit" which removes it into the dazzling splendor of the sun "via the canal of the vertical line of the center-post."

This predominant function of the ritual flags illustrates why they are made as lovely as possible, and are as costly as the finances of the oum'phor permit. The prices of some flags are as astronomical as the stars they symbolize. Some oum'phors have gone bankrupt paying for them.

When not in use, the flags are customarily leaned against the pé where they renew their psychic virtue; for they develop a formidable psychic power as soon as they are taken out of the inner oum'phor. This power is further increased, especially as the flag's recessional from the holy of holies is sometimes accompanied by a regular mob of people waving brilliantly colored scarfs and crowding the circuitous path of the flag in the oum'phor area.

The flags are carried by two houn'sihs, usually women, traditionally called co-drapeaux. These flag bearers surround a male houn'sih called la place or commandant la place, who guides their movements. Their movements are exciting, always in accordance with the magic system of a symbolism which requires that the ceremonial material be of an exceptional lightness, in accordance with the condition which naturally effects its "ravishment."

The ritual function of La Place can be understood from Genesis, which states that after Adam and Eve had tasted the forbidden fruit, God "drove out the man; and he placed at the east of the Garden of Eden cherubims and a flaming sword which turned every way, to keep the way of the tree of life." Therefore, "to keep the way" of the poteau-mitan, the Voodoo tradition requires La Place to brandish his machete or his sword across the oum'phor, starting from the east. The post is the arbre-sé or arbre-sec, the spiritual "tree of life," while the east is the door of the oum'phor which opens onto the peristyle.

As soon as La Place steps out of the oum'phor, he leads the co-drapeaux in a perfect performance of the ritual salutations addressed in hierarchic order first to the drums, the center-post, the officiating huon'gan or mam'bo, then to all the other houn'gans and mam'bos who may be present. Finally, a special salutation is given to distinguished guests, initiated or not, who are present though not actually participating in the ceremony.

After the salute to the drums and before the other salutations, La

Place leads the co-drapeaux outside to salute the reposoirs in the yard. During this time especially, the exhibition of the flags is particularly spectacular. The evolutions of the three participants reach a stage in which they become a veritable riot of multicolored silk, in which the ritual sword of La Place executes such a lacework of patterns in the air that it is a wonder how he always manages to keep from injuring anyone.

Sword of La Place

The sword itself also plays an important role in the ceremony. Magically, it is the emblem and the attribute of the Ogous, loas whose most prestigeous religious personification is St. James the Great. From this it necessarily follows that it is the Ogous who in the African tradition "ravish" transcendentally the ritual material.

The true name of La Place's sword is *ku-bha-sah*, a word that necessarily implies that "the greatest of the invisibles" (Bha) "has slain or abolished" (kou, ku) "all that which is material, all that which is the depths or the abyss" (sah). In short, it may be said that the movements of the ritual flags in Voodoo are a magical totality and summit. They encompass and epitomize Voodoo.

Because of the sword's action in abolishing the material substance, the *bha-sah* portion of the word *ku-bha-sah* signifies "cutting," while the sword of La Place is the ritual epitome of the sacrificial knives. It is also called the *Ogoubhasah* in that it is the counterpart of the staff of *Ogoubhatalah*. In Africa, La Place's sword has the name of "Father of Cutting Weapon," and it represents traditionally the best work of the ironsmith, since in the Voodoo tradition, it is the mystère who works iron (Ogou Fer) who reveals to men the secrets of Voodoo magic.

Actually this ritual sword should be engraved with geometric designs corroborating the basis of the physical and metaphysical architecture of the oum'phor, a custom now abolished, to all intents and purposes, in the oum-phor of Haiti. The African houn'gans regarded these designs as representing primarily the sun of Legba, the thunderstone or axe of Québiésou, and the triangles, which recall the conical form of the drums. Part of the blade is serrated to represent the progress of the ritual offerings, slain by the instrument of the Ogous, towards the celestial regions, which are their destination.

The sword, the machete, or the dagger of the Ogous represents the serpent Dan-Bah-Lah *(da, dan)* in wrought iron *(gou, ogou)*. For this reason, among the oracular signs of the magic alphabet the African sign of the Ogous is *gou-da* or *ogou-dan*. The sword is considered also ·to be the male organ of the mystère *Québiésou Dan Leh* (The Thunder). This weapon—knife, sword, machete, or dagger—is what kills *(okou)* the sacrificial victim. It is also called *okou-bha-sah,* and insofar as it is the rod of Québiésou or of the Thunder, it has a close connection with the center-post of the peristyle and the socle, the character of both of which is sexual, for Québiésou is an ancient Legba, one of the wisest of all the Legbas. This snake-weapon is therefore one of the most important factors in Voodoo.

Foods of Voodoo

A discussion of the favorite foods of the loas is fraught with difficulties and should not be based solely on Voodoo as practiced in Haiti. Nor should it be said dogmatically that the menus prepared in the Haitian ritual for the mystères are absolutely orthodox. What Voodoo orthodoxy usually means by the ritual feeding—*the magic trophology*—of the loas will be explained first. Then some notes will follow on the foods which Haitian cultists generally offer.

First, it must be remembered that all the ritual foods have their magical correspondence in the astral. Just as Erzulie loves perfume, Legba prefers the bones of the animal sacrifices, because these elements correspond to certain degrees of the atmosphere. For in Voodoo the ritual foods are offered in order to nourish, to enliven or fortify, and to make contact with the invisible powers. The better the ritual food is adapted to the loas' requirements, the greater the magical power immediately available.

It is therefore up to the Voodooist to learn the food preferences of the loas whom he invokes and whom he must consequently feed in order to have their power at his disposal. So, if Legba prefers bones but he is given tripe, he either gives a poor performance or else he fails altogether to do what is requested of him, because his potential astral correspondence has been poorly developed or not developed at all.

For the purpose of analogy to which we shall return presently, the sacrificial offering is always placed on the *crossroads* of a vèvè, or on whatever part of a ritual design represents the crossroads (since any cross formed by two straight intersecting lines is analogous to a crossroad) in order that its astral recipient will be more disposed to accept it.

Since the crossroads is geometrically and logically related to *Legba Ati Bon* (the Sun), the ritual fact alone proves that the person who makes the sacrificial offering joins, for his own practical purposes, the vertical forces of all astral space with the horizontal forces. For this reason Legba is referred to in some chants as *Legba Grand-Chemin* (Legba of the Highway) and *Maître Grand-Chemin* (Master of the Highway). The "highway" is, in principle and in essence, the *interferential nucleus* of the cross.

The depositing of the sacrifice on this geometric crossroads for its ensuing consignment to the astral-causal accords necessarily with all the scientific significance of the cross.

Since the cross and the square of the cross are formed respectively by two and by four separate squares, the Square (which is the *Grand Master* of the astral-causal) symbolizes the passive material of the sacrifice which has been rectified, organized, actuated, activated, and balanced by the person who places it at the crossroads of Legba, who is, accordingly, the master of the astral-causal.

In Voodoo, this magic crossroads is synthetized in the *barrier* because, like the crossing of the roads, the barrier opens the ways to permit passage. The following chant explains the concept of this opening of the ways of the astral by which the material of the rectified, organized, and balanced sacrifice will ascend:

Ati Bon Legba, ouvri barriè pou moin, ago yé!	Ati Bon Legba, open the barrier for me, ago yeh!
Voudoun Legba, ouvri barriè pou moin, pou moin ca rentré.	Voudoun Legba, open the barrier for me, so that I can re-enter.
L'heì m'a tounin, m'a remercié loa-yo.	When I return I shall thank the loas.

The African formula "Ago Yé!" is the nucleus of this chant, for it means *(Ago)* "attention," and *(Yé)* "to the soul," or "to the psyche represented by the sacrifice." It is the voodoo Mercury who conducts the soul from the visible to the invisibles, starting from the crossroads, and who then leads the invisibles to the crossroads to receive the sacrifice. The Voodoo Mercury has the name of *Simbi,* a loa of many forms. He is the *conductor of souls* who leads the souls of the dead in all directions bordered by the four magic orients of the cross. He is the Messiah of Legba, the messenger of the sun. Simbi corresponds to the hermetic Mercury of the cabalistic alchemy of the ritual sacrifice. Thus, he is simultaneously Hermes and Mercury—a boundary-god or milestone-god of roads and highways, as well as a genius of points of crossing. Simbi is the creative principle of the seminal vesicle because, in the Voodoo tradition, Legba, as centerpost, is himself the principle of the magic wand and the spinal marrow. In the science of Voodoo as elsewhere, the sacrifice principle is identified with the human principle, the greatest of all sacrifices when placed upon the cross. The analogy of "man-and-cross" then becomes the phallic form attributed to the mystère Ati Bon Legba.

The forming of a cross in order to utilize its power as a force of Nature requires the formula of the loa which represents the most powerful of divine intercessions: the intercession *"grand-maître—maître-et-maîtresse"* (grand master—master-and-mistress), formed by the African trinity:

Dan-Bha-Lah   GRAND MAÎTRE
LEGBA or LAH   MAÎTRE
ERZULIE   MAÎTRESSE

The magic formula of this intercession is therefore

(Jesus) YE-SOU: YE– = soul, psyche,
                        the magic *mirror*
          SOU = male, or creator
(Christ)   the   Cross: produced by the special crossing
                        of Danbhalah and Erzulie

The "mirror" is the definitive attribute of Erzulie's adornment and represents Erzulie herself—*Erzulie Mirror Zé* or *Erzulie Miroir Zo*—(meaning the mirror of Legba on the "point" of Jupiter the Thunderer, the father of Simbi); while the philological aspect of the soul reveals that the mystère Erzulie is a "silver mirror" (the moon) crossed with Yésou, or "gold" (the Sun). Therefore, because of the spacial crossing of the sacrificial cross of Voodoo, Erzulie is the loa of riches. In Voodoo this means the same thing as omniscience. This astral aspect of the soul through sacrifice indicates therefore why Voodoo is an animistic cult. Furthermore, the following chant selected from the liturgical repertory of Voodoo clearly suggests this problem:

Grande Aï-Zan, salué Legba!	Grande Aï-Zan (who represents
À l'heu qu'il é	the purity of Legba),
l'argent cassé roche.	salute Legba!
M'a pé mandé coument nous yé?	Now silver breaks rock.
Salué Legba.	I am asking how you are?
Créoles sondé miroi Legba.	Salute Legba.
Aï-Zan vié, vié,	Créoles, sound Legba's mirror.
Vié Legba,	Aï-Zan, old one, old one,
Créoles sondé mirori Legba.	Old Legba,
Legba vié, vié.	Créoles, sound Legba's mirror.
Créoles, sondé miroi Ati Bon Legba!	Legba, old one, old one. Créoles, sound Ati Bon Legba's mirror.

The significance of the expression sondé miroi, which occurs in many chants, and may be translated freely "plumb the depths of the mirror," or "search in the mirror," is one of the greatest secrets of Voodoo.

There are certain traditional correlations between the mystères and animals which clarify the animating principle—the very soul-principle—of Voodoo magic, and illustrate it in accordance with the principles of universal magic rather than with those of any dubious tradition. They also reveal through the very animal character of the loas the sacrifices preferred by them as animals (unless for contrary occult reasons the animal sacrifices be among the "forbidden rituals").

Danbhalah (Yé Dan-Gbé)	snake, snake's eggs
Legba	lion, white sheep (bones and marrow)

Aï-dan ....snake (revealing the character of the snake which the Virgin crushes underfoot, or "eats"); white pigeons

Erzulie ...."aziza" or "azili" snake (which corresponds to mirrors, perfumes, toothpastes, powders, silk cloth, lace, etc., because this type of snake signifies "cosmic adornment" or the "purification of sacrificial matter")

Agassou (Ati-A-Sou) ......royal leopard (the guardian-loa of the Dahomean Voodoo Tradition)

Loko Ati-Sou ....lizard, agama

Ogou-Fer ....red bull (the color of fire)

Agoueh-R-Oyo ....bull, sheep (black or white, depending upon the purposes of the magic)

Guédé Z'aringnin ....spider-crab

Aï-Zan Avélé Kéthé ....crab

Assatò (largest of the drums) ....crab

Assatò or Azinto Micho To-Kpo Voudoun .... alligator, crocodile (mystère of Haitian Independence who supervised the strategy of the Rada loas during the ceremonies of the Bois-Caïman and the Trou-Caïman)

The Voodoo sacrifice leads to a comprehension of the cabalistic idea of crucifixion. However, the animal which personifies each loa does not always suffice for the accomplishment of its magic, especially because Haitian Voodoo has lost part of its recollection of these important astro-animal identifications. The magic menu of the loas therefore is broadened to include other food offerings more available for ceremonial presentation, because of the fact that all the traditional ones are not available in Haiti. Consequently, the loas' menu is at once simpler and more complex. Here are a few examples:

Aï-Zan: green bananas, white rice, white glazed cakes, white desserts, white syrup, pure water, sweet liqueurs, pumpkins, yams, tayo malangas, essence of cinnamon, star anise, vanilla, white and brown poultry, sweet fruit of lianas; assorossi, calebassi, grenadines.

Danbhalah Wédo: corn flour, wheaten flour, olive oil, castor oil, cakes, Cola Champagne (a Haitian soft drink, substituted homophonically for cola nuts, the divine attribute of the greatest of the African mystères: Apha or Pha, whose geographic counterpart is Ifa or Ifé and La Ville Aux Camps), various fruits, champagne, orgéat served in white cups, pastry on white plates, sweetened coffee, an egg (preferably a snake's egg) upon a white saucer of white flour, white wine, white desserts or those prepared with milk, pure milk, and powdered sugar.

In Voodoo the sun is personified by Legba Ati Bon (Legba Tree-of-the-Good). While Legba represents in anatomy the vertebral column (hence his preference for the bones and marrow), he is also identified with the vertebral bones of the oum'phor—the poteau-mitan. He is also represented by the little magic snake bones (which in turn suggest the bones of ancestors) which decorate the asson with which the houn'gans and mam'bos direct the ceremonies, dances, and ritual chorus. Legba or his post is therefore the "column" of the oum'phor—*boa-la-couleuvre*—from which the columns of the other temples—*Bohas*—will be derived.

This wood-principle, or Bohas-principle of the Voodoo temple consists not only of the post (the Sun) but also of the loa which magically guards it—Ati Dan Lbo Loko.

Because in the Voodoo tradition Legba Ati Bon is considered the greatest medical doctor and the greatest magician, he claims the same tree (ati-n) as Papa Loko Ati Dan: the *médecinier béni*. His corresponding animal, analogous to Loko, is the lizard *(anolis)*, which may be interpreted in the sense of the "sacred cycle." The "sacred cycle" is the astral crossroads which the two extremities of the vertical line of the vèvè reproduce in the form of a crossed circle. The *anolis* of the "sacred cycle" then indicates both the principal food offering of Legba as well as Christ of the crucifixion. For this reason the expansible elastic membrane under the throat of the lizard, which he uses to produce sound, symbolizes both the *word* and the *sun.*

In the sun-earth occultism, the harvest is symbolized by the yam or "manger-yam," fresh yams plus other products of the soil, as well as dried fish representing water which is blessed or "virginized" by the sun because the fish is the symbol of Christ when it is dried in a charcoal fire. Now, in the symbolism of the universal ritual *harvest* is the same as the *first labors* of the Earth. This solar-agricultural synthesis of the earth is sacrificially offered in communion or in transubstantiation to the mystères as the first sacrifice, and it is due to the importance of Christ that the manger-yam is the ceremony which opens the door to all the loas and to all the faithful, Legba being the "principal door" of the ancient rituals, that is to say, the magic portal of the voodoo ritual. Thus the houn'gan sacrifices the yam, in order to sacrifice the first of the best harvest of the land, exactly as the priest proceeds to the sacrifice of the mass or the body of Christ (the Voodoo yam), which is offered in transubstantiation, and as Golgotha is concerned with the sacrifice of the Messiah.

The yam, as first and principal fruit of the land, is therefore traditionally considered to be illuminated by the cardinal point which is the East or Orient of the Voodoo orientation; for this point of the ritual orientation is the "gateway of Legba."

The first fruits thus harvested and offered in communion as the Voodoo *maza* (*mazda* or *Ahourah Mäzda* of the Persians) give birth to the loas which bathe in the fire at Christmas, in order to symbolize the first labors of the Earth: the mystères *Boum'ba Maza*, who represent the Messianic voyage or boat *(boum'ba)* of Christ (Massah, Messiah, Missah, Maza) as "sacrifice" or "victim." Since Christ is the anointed, the houn'gan generously sprinkles with oil the piles of first fruits piled up before the Voodoo altars.

In the oum'phors that have preserved the tradition of the yams, the ground of the peristyle is completely covered with a bed of banana leaves on the day of the ceremony. The food offerings of the *coucher-yam* are served to the houn'sihs seated around this immense green covering. The yams are presented to them on white plates, and when they have been eaten by the houn'sihs, the rite proceeds to the "voyage to Ifé." It commences with the following chant.

Baco-sou entré,
Baco-sou rivé
Dèdè, O Savalou

Ogan, Dèdè ogan Savalou,
Dèdè ogan, ogan é é é é é é é é

The bed of green leaves is thought to represent the surface of water
which the magic bark of the loas crosses to reach the city of Ifé. Consequently, the Voodoo initiates proceed to travel on it just as regular
ships would. They salute the three points—south, centerpost, and west
—with a mystic kiss upon the ground which is laid the ritual leaves.
Then they lie down at the west. They roll themselves one after the
other, but never two at the same time, from west to east. They are
accompanied by the houn'gan, asson in hand. When they reach a
candle lit on the east side, where for the most part they usually stop
on their own accord, they lie there a moment stretched out upon the
ground lying on one side. Then they return, rolling themselves again
to a candle lit on the west side where the houn'gan helps them to
their feet.

One matter is especially important: the houn'sihs are invariably
possessed by mystères during the crossing in such a way that it is
always a mystère coming from Ifé, the East, which helps him to his
feet. It is therefore evident that the houn'sih, by rolling on the ground
to simulate this magic crossing, imitates not only the rolling and whit-
ening of the waves, but travels to the East (or Ifé) to obtain a re-
newal of psychic powers.

Inasmuch as the water is ruled by the mystère Agoueh R Oyo, the
ritual chant ending the ceremony is:
Bha roulé, Agoueh-tò . . .
Some of the initiates then roll up the leaves which they will bury
in a secret way while the choir of houn'sih canzos continues to chant
to the rhythmic beating of the drums:

Bha roulé, Agoueh-Tò!
Bha roulé, Agoueh-Tò!

The Banana Tree

According to the orthodox tradition of Voodoo, supported by the
universal tradition, the banana tree is the tree of the first and greatest
of the houn'gans (Adam), just as it is the tree of the first and most
learned of the mam'bos (Eve, whom voodooists call Erzulie). Now

the Tree of Adam is identified in the traditional magic, with the fig tree of the scriptures.

Just so, the leaves of the banana tree conduct the houn'sihs, the houn'gans, and the mam'bos to Ifé (the heavens, the Earthly Paradise), in the Voodoo rites, because the fig tree conceals the center-post. The Voodoo initiates claim that fruit of knowledge, which the serpent Danbhalah offers to the mam'bos, is a banana. They identify necessarily the banana, which enters very often into the composition of the ritual foods, with the substance of the sun seen above the Voodoo *pés*, and which is dominated by the traditional serpent of the oum'phors. For this reason the banana leaves lead to Ifé in *Afrique Guinin*, for the sun which is pictured above the voodoo altars represents not only the mysterious city of Ifé or (La Ville Aux Camps), but also the center of the initiation.

In the Holy Scriptures as in Voodoo, "evil bananas" or "evil *figues*" (*figues-bananes*) signify "evil initiates," "faithless initiates," an allusion to the cursed fig tree of the Bible, while the "good *figues-bananes*" are the initiates who faithfully serve the loas, and who honor and respect the mystères, so that in a larger sense, the "accursed fig tree" of the Bible or the "accursed banana tree" of Voodoo is the church or the oum'phor badly served: the oum'phor without center-post, the church without Christ!

By analogy this means that the reputation of the banana tree makes its fruit not only the most useful of vegetables, but renders a certain serpent called the *bramine* (because of the term *brahmin*, which signifies "priest" and "doctor of religion") exceptionally fond of touching both the shadow and the fruit of the banana tree. This serpent feeds upon bananas, to mention the tradition, in order to be able to live more than 100 years!

Furthermore, as the centerpost is the Voodoo sun, and inasmuch as the solar life renews itself by its daily rising and setting, the banana tree never ceases to renew itself by its shoots. Its perpetual outgrowings symbolize eternal life. The banana tree is, moverover, like the gods, hermaphroditic as to its flowers.

The rising and setting of the voodoo Sun (East and West in the magic orientation indispensable to every sort of supernatural operation) agrees with the beliefs held by learned mythologists relative to the mystère *Brahmâ*, who owes his name to a type of serpent which enjoys eating *figues-bananes*. For, like the mystère of the serpents

Danbhalah Wédo and Aida Wédo of Voodoo, the mystère Brahmâ derives his mastery of magic from the cosmos through the concept of life
and death. Papa Legba, as center-post, is accordingly *Para-Brahma*,
or *Papa-Brahma*, the single line of the post, the "Sole Being" of all
the religious doctrines having the form of the post, the divine cause
of all the mysteries, the cosmic essence whence come and whither return all the loas and all the beings subordinated to them. The magic
signature of this single line of the post (or of the banana tree) is a
triangle with a circle in its center. The triangle represents Danbhalah-
Legba-Erzulie (the holy trinity of Voodoo), revealing the magic
trinity existing in the sun, the astral symbol of the banana tree, of the
figuier-béni, and of the post. The circle in the center of the triangle
is the Sun-Child (Child Jesus of Voodooism), and this is why the sun
is pictured above the Voodoo *pe* as son and as first manifestation of
Para-Brahma: Brahmâ, whose two other hypostases are Vich-nou
and Shiva. This being the case, it is evident that Para-Brahma or Para-
Brahmin, while recalling the bramine serpent of the banana tree, corresponds to the serpent Danbhalah Wédo, and Brahmâ himself, to
Legba Ati-Bon, who personifies the magic powers of the houn'gans
and mam'bos.

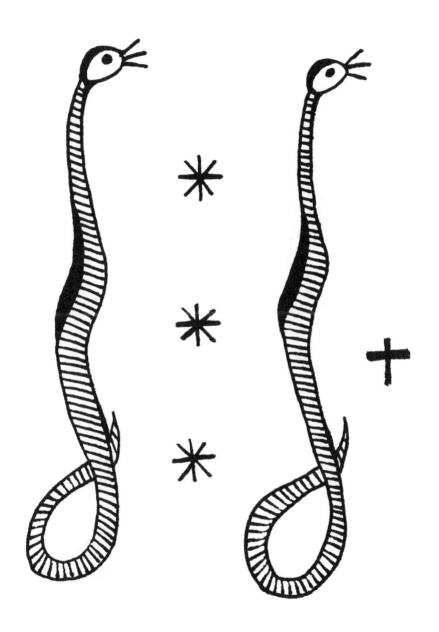

Vèvè of Danbhalah and Aïda We'do.

Vèvè of Aizan used in a Rada rite.

Vèvè of Ti Pierre Dantor used in a Pethro rite.

Vèvè of Legba.

Vèvè of Ogou Fer used in a Nago rite.

Vèvè of Linglessou bossin-sang (Linglessou bucket-of-blood)

Vèvè of Brise.

Vèvè of Simbi.

Vèvè of Erzulie.

Vèvè of Milo-Can (several spirits).

Vèvè traced around the ceremonial hole
where the offerings must be burned.

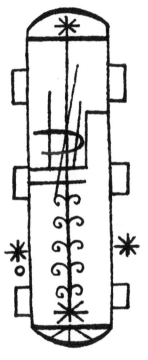

Vèvè in the form of a coffin for magic treatments, following the summoning of Brise.

Vèvè traced around a ceremonial hole over
which is the table of ritual offerings.

Vèvè of Azaca, loa of Agriculture.

Vèvè of Ossangne Negre Goue-sih Malor, the father of Legba.

Vèvè of Ossangne.

Vèvè of Danbhalah-la-flambeau (Danbhalah-the-torch).

Vèvè of Agoueh, spirit of water.

Vèvè of Grand Bois of Ife, representing
the occult power of the woods.

Ritual diagram of the boulez-zains-les-morts, also ouan-zain: pots boiling for the dead.

Vèvè of Erzulie Dantor.

5

Sounds, Rhythms, Chants, and Prayers

THE musical instruments, chants, dances, and prayers that are an integral part of Voodoo and of Voodoo ceremonies each bear symbolic interrelationships that must be clearly understood to comprehend Voodoo itself.

The Ogan

The *ogan*—an instrument resembling a flattened bell without a clapper—is struck in rhythm with an iron rod by a musician called the *ogantier*. In most Voodoo ceremonies its insistent rhythm is piercing and deafening, and the listener usually wishes it were silent, the better to catch the fascinating rhythm of the drums. Not infrequently it is the ogantier's metallic beating upon the ogan that leads off the other instruments. However, there are exceptions to this practice, as sometimes the orchestra dispenses with the ogan.

In the Voodoo tradition the ogan is basically the chromatic director of the ritual orchestra. Its mystère is *Ogan-sih Hwé-Do*. Its beat rhythmically controls the sacred Chromatic. Its virtue lies in the correspondence which exists between its rhythmo-choregic function and the esoteric formula implied in the word *o-gan*. For this formula signifies "chief of the magic circle," or "ruler of the ceremonial material."

The Triangle

The triangle is an iron instrument, triangular in form. The triangle finds its counterpart shape in the triangular niche inset in the masonry of the socle of the poteau-mitan. Sometimes, however, the triangular niche is merely painted on the socle or abyss. This geometric correspondence, when referring to the magical organization of the ritual and of the ritual Chromatic, definitely signifies that the abysses are opened by the triangular form, with Danbhalah Wédo, Erzulie, and Legba at each of the three points of the triangle.

By the fact that the musical triangle opens the abysses, it opens also the ritual water symbolized by the socle set beneath the post. The socle, then, represents Erzulie on the "point" of the abyss, provided the socle is not "open" by having the Masonic triangular niche painted on or inset in its side. But if the socle of the post does contain the triangle, either inset or painted, then Erzulie is said to "walk" upon the "point" of the "brilliant ascension of the Moon and of Venus."

The magic role of this chromatic instrument consists in "opening the path of the air." Thus, as an orchestral instrument which directs the ritual airs, it opens analogically (as mystère or loa of analogy— of the magic analogy of the ritual air) the path which must conduct all material employed in the ceremonies, as well as the practitioners themselves, into the astral heights of the atmospheric air. For this reason the Universal Tradition calls the triangle the *Luminous Delta*.

We may note that, insofar as the Voodoo cult is concerned, this triangular luminous delta, which is such an outstanding feature of the ritual orchestra, is reflected in the curious but most appropriate shape that the initiates have given the drumstick used with the drum that represents orchestrally the light and the magic powers of the sun, namely the voudoun Legba Ati-Bon. The form of the stick used to beat the second drum (the middle one of the three Rada drums) is that of a "D", the Roman form of the Greek delta.

Just as the Voodoo Legba—as the sun—represents the Orient, universal Masonry, which has its source in the masonry socle of the poteau-mitan, places its Esoteric Triangle or Luminous Delta above and behind the head of the throne of the Venerable of the Lodge. Similarly to the placement of the triangle in the lodges, the Voodoo tradition bestows the title of *principal maître-tête* upon the sun (Legba Ati-Bon), by reason of the fact that while all the other loas may be *maître têtes*, Legba is above them, as the sun is above the powers of all the constellations.

In the oum'phor, the form of the musical triangle traditionally appears again above the pé, or altar. It is not surprising, then, that, although the equilateral triangle is altered, for hermetic reasons, from the normal form of the musical instrument, the Greek Geometric Tradition, as revealed by Plato and Pythagoras, holds that the best religious altars preferably have the form of the right triangle. Just so, the base of this right triangle (the hypotenuse) is the scientific base of the altar. The following explanation is offered the uninitiated: "The reason for the importance of the right triangle is that 'the square on the hypotenuse is equal to the sum of the squares on the other two sides'."

It is easy to find this algebraic and geometric formula again and again in the architecture of the Voodoo peristyle. The equilateral triangle "Danbhalah-Legba-Erzulie" already exists in the masonry of the socle. Through geometric transcendence it becomes, by duplication of itself, a rectangle, the form concealed within the right triangle —the classic rectangle which is generally the form of the peristyle.

It also is worth noting that through Danbhalah, Legba, and Erzulie, the musical triangle suggests the divine Trinity: the Father, Son, and Holy Ghost. Doubtless for this reason Xenocrates used to compare divinity to an equilateral triangle. The Freemasons who are said to have had their origin in the Voodoo socle of Legba, have the oculate triangle in the masonry pediments of their lodges exactly as the Voodoo adepts did before them, and still do, in Haiti, upon the perfect circle of the socle of their *poteau-soleil* (sun-post). The eye in the center of the triangle stands for the elevation of Erzulie by Legba.

A curious circumstance, accidental or otherwise, may be noted in the fact that in Voodoo the apex of the musical and Masonic triangle is held by the mystère Danbhalah Wédo who, in the African cabal, is called Danbhalah-Yéwé (or more exactly Ié-H-Wé), while in Freemasonry the Tetragrammaton, represented alphabetically by I. E.

V. E., occupies the ocular center of the triangle. Alexander West-
phal, the author of works on Masonry, declares that the origin of the
Tetragrammaton of the lodges is under dispute, and that no one really
knows the correct pronunciation of the letters, despite all the variations adopted by devotees of solar cults (such as Io, Ia, Ya, Yaveh,
Iého-schuah, Jeshuah, Jeho-vah, Joschoueh, Josué, Jesus, and Jesus-
Christ). However, Voodooists have always known how to pronounce
them, for the simple reason that they realize that the eye in the triangle symbolizes "Erzulie chromatically ravished by Legba and that
one of the Ethiopian or solar names of Legba Atibon is Yé-Ch-Ou.
The eye in the triangle is then a synthesis of ritual knowledge
through the solar scheme of Voodoo, as a result of which initiates
"see" the light proceed from the sun (Legba) under the form of
Erzulie or one of her manifestations. At the same time, it is a synthesis of Danbhalah-Yéwé in the astral–causal. In Voodoo, the astral-
causal is the dark abyss of the socle of Legba converted into a "basin
filled with water," since the abysses are the "depths of the water." In
this aspect Erzulie is called "Mistress of the Water."

The Drums

The batteries of drums, whose magic rhythm is set by the chromatic
ogan and the triangle, form the major attraction of Voodoo in the eyes
of tourists who attend the ceremonies as spectators. Nothing inspires
more wonder than the drums because of their splendid conical shapes
and the fascinating gestures of the *houn'tôrguiers*, or drummers.
The patronymic mystère of the initiates who beat the drums is
Papa-Houn'thor, whose name is *Ima-Da-Govi*. They are under occult
submission to the mystère *Mam'bo Delai Medeh*, referred to in the
following song: "*Eyïa, houn'to-a he! Delaï commandé* . . . (Eyïa, the
drummer, hey! Delaï, give your command . . .)."
Through the preceding explanations about the ogan and the triangle you have learned that the musical instruments form a theological whole. In the oum'phor, the ogan, the triangle, and the drums represent the equivalent of all the astral atmospheres from the pyrosphere
(or central fire of the earth) to the nucleosphere, the chromosphere,
and the photosphere. These are the three atmospheric zones of Legba
—the sun. More particularly (and by reason of chemical magic con-

nected with the sacrificial ritual), the ogan, the drums, and the triangle are related to the solar chromosphere, while the sacred dances around the post which are inspired by the music are associated with the atmosphere of the solar nucleus.

A full consideration of the scientific constitution of the drums and their esoteric interpretation in Voodoo would be too advanced for the present work. However, we may describe the physical composition of several traditional orchestras of African origin that lend an African coloring to the religious history of Haitian Voodoo. The three classical batteries of drums are the Rada, the Pethro, and the Congo.

The Rada battery is composed of three drums that chromatically recombine the three atmospheres of the sun (that is, of the mystère Legba—for Legba is the quickening power behind Voodooism). Listed according to size and solar designation they are:
  (1) The *Manman,* related to the Chromosphere.
  (2) The *Second,* related to the Photosphere.
  (3) The *Bou-Lah,* related to the solar nucleus.

Because of their solar relationships and their resemblance in temperament to the Rada mystères, the Rada drums form the most brilliant battery of drums employed in Voodoo.

The word *Rada,* when analyzed and traced back to its geographical and mystical origins, reveals more clearly the significance of the drums of the same name. "Rada" is a simpler form of "Arada," the equivalent of "Allada," and its true sense is "Allah-Da," from which Voodoo very scientifically but very simply derives its serpent *Da(n).* This is, moreover, the serpent of Judaism, according to the Bible, for the Voodooist has only to reread carefully the testament of Jacob to find it, both under the form of the mystical serpent which is Dan-Bha-Lah, and under the other mystical form of "magic powers"—the Lion which personifies Legba. To the Voodooist the Koran itself proves the existence of the serpent not only by the word *Allah (Allah-Da),* but by the serpent *Legba,* which is a perfect translation of *Al-Lah-Dah,* by reason of the meaning of the drum *Bou-Lah.*

Consider now the two drums of the Pethro rite. They are related especially to the awful atmosphere of the solar nucleus. They are the so-called demonic, even cannibalistic drums, not through their own nature alone, but simply because their temperament, being of high temperature, renders them very difficult to control in magical operations. Consequently they are dangerous.

The larger of the two drums is identified with the thunderbolt. Its mystère is the Haitian voudoun *Québiésou Dan Leh* (the Dahomean *Hévio-Zo*, who is the Zeus of the Greeks). This dreadful mystère, otherwise as beneficent as he is dreadful, provided he is "served" correctly, is the guardian of the drums of the oum'phor, the divine and thundering guardian of the pé or the altar stone. He is the "chief of the thunder," or the mystère *Aga Tonnerre*, called *Aga-Ou Tonnerre* because of one of his numerous metamorphoses. The larger of the two Pethro drums "walks" astrologically upon the *"points-chauds"* (hot-points) of the planet Jupiter, which corresponds to the loa *Québiésou Dan Leh.*

The second, or smaller, Pethro drum is necessarily the complementary opposite of the first, representing, accordingly, the region of the cosmos that hears or receives the "bolt" of thunder. This region of the cosmos is Guinea, which for Voodoo traditionalists signifies "the extremity of the world."

The first drum is identified sidereally with the Southern portion of the sky, the second with the Northern portion which, in Voodoo terms, is "ruled" by the mystère *Sakbha Lah Tha Vovo Lih Vo*. In Haiti this mystère is known under the greatly altered form of *Guédé Sa Bha Lah*, a loa of the cemetery who reveals those diseases and impurities which are properly treated in the oum'phor by the Jupiter of Voodoo.

In the Congo rite there may be two drums or the battery of drums also may contain three other drums which, except for very slight differences, are the same as the Rada drums, and their names are practically the same. These three are called:

(1) The largest—the *Manman.*
(2) The middle-sized—the *Grondez.*
(3) The smallest—the *Ka-Tha-Bou.*

The *grondez* is used for the *second* of the Rada drums, and its name links it with the "tonnerre" (thunder) of the Pethro battery, while the *Katabou* is used for the Rada *Bou-Lah.*

In addition to the previously discussed Voodoo drums, the largest drum of all is the *Assato*. The magic power of this drum is limitless; wherefore, in accordance with this unlimited power, it is not played upon by merely one or even two drumsticks but "by more than a thousand," according to the claims of its devotees. Furthermore, the formidable character of its power requires that during the ritual it be beaten only by adepts who are possessed by the loas: "Let there be as many drumsticks as there are 'saints;' let there be as many 'saints' as there are drumsticks beating ceremonially!"

The full significance of the Voodoo drums can only be understood by considering their origin. As a geometric consequence of the idea of "Earth-sex," the drum membrane or drumhead is believed to have been the skin forming the external ear of the serpent Danbhalah, wherefore snakes no longer have visible ears. By beating the voodoo drum, the drummer makes himself heard by Danbhalah via a direct, analogical pathway—the drumhead, which is the ear of the greatest of all the mytères; Dan Gbé Tò. Drums differ in form according to rite, because the geometric system upon which their construction is based represents not only a rite but also the dialect spoken by the "nation" of loas of that rite, as well as by the devotees of that "nation" of loas.

For this reason the Rada drums are the "tribal geometry" of the voodoo *langage* spoken by the Aradas. The form of these drums, like that of the others, is determined by the common language, and has been supernaturally revealed to the earliest initiates in exactly the same way and through the same tradition as the form of the tabernacle was revealed to Moses.

All of these traditional, fundamental ideas strongly prove the existence of an insoluble bond between the snake interred in the primordial earth in the form of a cone-shaped drum and the Voodoo *pé* whose form is that of a slightly raised tomb or burial vault. The snake has its abode within the stonework of the *pé* because it was interred in the earth (in Ifé or in Ville Aux Camps) with the alliance-stones which are rediscovered in the form of golden finger-rings belonging to Maîtresse Erzulie Fréda Dahomey Tocan Miroizé Zagaza. The gold of these rings represents the sun. They are found on antique drums as large hoops of red copper because of the fact that, in magic terms, copper is the true metal of Erzulie (Venus) and also because the copper hoops give the drums better resonance.

The drums themselves must from time to time "make a trip to Ifé" in order to renew their supply of magic force. In this case they are said to be "put to bed," or "fed." These ceremonies are the *coucher-tambours* ("putting the drums to bed") and the *baille-tambours-manger* ("feeding the drums"). To "put the drums to bed" is the same thing as sending initiates of the various degrees to Ifé in order to have their degrees conferred upon them.

In the ceremony the sacred drums are taken from the great crossed circle which will be their oum'phor—the oum'phor in which they are beaten—in order to recline them upon the bed of banana leaves supposed to represent *Guinin.* There a candle is lit on each of them. Not only the drums, but also all the other cult instruments, such as the ogans, have to make this voyage. During the time they are on their bed they are given something to eat. Ritual food and liqueurs are sprinkled over them and upon the designs that represent them to give them strength.

While the drums are lying down a distribution is made to the chickens about to be sacrificed of the sacrificial food offerings placed both upon the vèvès and upon the drums themselves. Then these chickens are passed and repassed over the houn'gan and the kneeling houn'-sihs for a communication of powers. Then the birds are sacrificed to the instruments. Once killed they are placed upon the vèvès whence they will later be taken to be prepared. The mam'bo gives a drink of alcohol to the reclining drums by sprinkling the liquor over them. She casts the water in the four holes surrounding the post, also some coffee, the food-offerings of the sacrifice, as well as the liqueurs. The houn'sihs come to worship at these holes, kissing the ground before them, placing coins in them, at the same time pronouncing certain prayers while kneeling. The candles are extinguished and placed in the holes, which are then filled. The drums are covered with white sheets symbolizing the purifying atmosphere of the city of Ifé in Guinin.

Then the machete is stuck in the ground before the drums, and the ritual flags are placed over the white sheets which cover them as though they were dead.

The drums are of necessity "put to bed" to the singing of the *bô-houn'*, or funeral chants, and the audience all at one becomes very sad because the "putting to bed" of the drums is not only a departure but a new death: the gods of the wood are supposed to effect the crossing of the water, just like the sheep of Agoueh that is white like the white sheet which cover the drums, to go to Africa and return from there with powers renewed.

With reference to Ifé, the place where they go as source of the Voodoo tradition, with reference to the mystère of the drums called *Houn'tor,* and with reference to the funerary meaning of the ceremony, the following are the chants that accompany the crossing:

O Houn'tò mrin!
Côté ou pr'allez?
Ago! Nannan Wédo . . .
Houn'tò mrin, papa mrin,
Côté ou pr'allez?
E, ago é!
Ago! Nannan Wédo . . .
Houn'tò! Rhélez Houn'tò é,
Papa Sobo
Qui! Hountò-à . . .
Ladogouessan.
Sobagui Sobo, nous là;
Lò n'a mouri,
N'a quitté répos pou yo.

Eya, Bô-Gan,

Gô-Gan Ilé (Ifé)!
Houn'gan, ago!
Lé-Guédé, Bô N'gan,
Voyiez rhéler Bogan.
O, Man-Yanvalou Micho!

Oh, my Houn'tor!
Where are you going?
Ago! Nannan Wédo . . .
My Houn'tor, my father,
Where are you going?
E, ago é!
Ago! Nannan Wédo . . .
Houn'tor! Call the Houn'tor,
Papa Sobo
Yes! The Houn'tor
Ladogouessan.
Sobagui Sobo, we are here;
It is only when we shall die,
that we shall give them rest.

Eya, Houn'gan, maker of talismen,
Bô-Gan Ifé!
Houn'gan, ago!
Lé-Guédé, Bô Gan-Gan,
Have Bogan called.
O, Man-Yanvolou Micho!

The voyage of the white sheep of Agoueh R Oyo, the drums, the initiates, and the houn'gans to Ifé is a resurrection of the flesh offered in sacrifice in all species. In the Voodoo tradition this voyage renews the magic powers properly so-called as much as the administrative and governmental powers of the society. The tradition teaches that it pertains to the Voodoo society and to society in general, a fact which shows why the two are closely associated in the peristyle, for the aim of this mysterious voyage among the loas is to see again the ancestors who are withdrawn into the stars of the vèvès by death. These are the ancestors who retain the powers as well as give them back.

The drums synthetize the principle of the resurrection by the wood and by the skin, shown in Egyptian symbolism by the burial of Osiris wrapped in a skin and inside the trunk of a tree. For this reason, in ordinary teaching, the creation is represented by three skins fastened together above and held up by a solar disk. This sort of trident-form, tied above and held by the sun symbolizes the androgenous or par-

thenogenic function of water pictured by the trident or the three skins
and by the fire which is pictured as the sun.

From this it follows, through the syncretism of the cabalas, that the
ti-ké-nou or the "resurrection by the skin" of the Egyptian rites is
equal to the three drums of the Rada orchestra which symbolize the
three planes of the Universal Soul or the three divine Hypostases. The
following are the parallels:

Voodoo	*Egyptian-Jewish*
FIRST drum (1st skin)	= NECHAMAH (Soul-Spirit)
MANMAN drum (2nd skin)	= NEPHESCH (Soul-Liver)
BOULAH drum (3rd skin)	= ROUACH (Soul-Heart)

The Egyptian *tikénou* reclines, moreover, in or upon the skin, to
renew itself spiritually, just as the drummer, the houn'gan, the
mam'bo, or the houn'sihs of Voodoo lie down and roll themselves upon
the drum in order to renew their forces. For this reason the arm of the
Voodoo drummer represents the Alpha and Omega of the Universal
cabala, while his hand is the Roman D, the Jewish daleth, and the
Greek delta, all of which relates the musical performance of the drums
to the following occult identifications:

$$A - O = \text{Divine Act}$$
$$D \quad\;\; = \text{Human Act}$$

Now, as the Rada formula signifies sun (Râ) serpent (Da), it is the
life-giving principle of the sun which "recharges" by means of the
drumskin the initiates who roll themselves against the cylindrical
wood.

The Voodoo Chorus

The voodoo chorus is composed of houn'sihs, both male and female,
and directed by the *houn'guénicon,* who usually is a woman. The
houn'guénicon is, after the houn'gan, the most conspicuous person in
the peristyle. She leads the chorus, "sending" the chants and performing the dance movements, moving back and forth in front of the
houn'sihs, and waving her arms and hands about in such a way that
they resemble branches of a tree stirred by the wind. She conducts
the ceremonies along with the houn'gan, and her function is basically

concerned with the magic of sound by which the loas are "called" and made to "descend" and be present or to participate in the ritual services. Her function is all the more important, in the peristyle and elsewhere, in that she is the one who "sends" the ritual chants necessary for making contact with the loas in the astral. All chromatic magic rests upon her knowledge. She is the sonic soul of the peristyle. Moreover, in view of her knowledge, relative chiefly to liturgical chant, her title is explained in accordance with traditional etymology as follows:

houn' = "drum" (or any instrument of sacred music)
-gué-, or *-jé-* = "supposed to be"
-nukon-, or *-nikon-* = "the first"
voudoun-sih = "*houn'sihs*," or "women"

The houn'sihs who form the chorus are classically robed in white, preferably in white linen. This rule is not observed, however, if the service is celebrated exclusively for the Pethro loas. In this case the houn'sihs may be dressed completely in red. They have even been known to wear purple in a Voodoo service in honor of Ogou Bhalin'dio. But for services of no special importance, houn'sihs usually wear their everyday clothes.

The chorus sings the ritual chants which, like the other geometric and chromatic elements of Voodoo, are related to occult forces of the air, the atmosphere, and the astral. The chants which the houn'sihs, under the leadership of the houn'guénicon, "send," magnetically attract the mystères lurking in the area around the Voodoo ceremony. The ritual chants composed for this purpose go out into the atmosphere to search out the loas and magnetize them. Having found them, they magnetize them as forces of the invisible, obliging them to come and incarnate themselves "in the heads" of their "horses." This is the primary ritual function of the chorus of *houn'sih can-zos.* Its next most important function is to assist the battery of drums in getting the incarnated loas as well as the houn'sihs not in a state of possession to dance.

In the occultism of Voodoo, the ritual chorus of the houn'sih can-zos represents one of the most important factors. In the metabolism of the magic of sacrifice, the airs sung by the houn'sihs are what aid the blood of the animal victims and the essence of the food or other offerings in rising via the mystères to their astral destination. The chorus plays this most important role since, by reason of a series of philosophi-

cal and chemical analogies it is identified cabalistically with the "heart
of the mystère Erzulie." Now since Erzulie is the wife of Legba, the
houn'sihs of the chorus are, all of them, necessarily wives of Legba,
that is to say, wives of the astro-biological system of the cult. Consequently, the person who leads the chorus—the houn'guénicon—is the
principal wife of Legba, as Legba in this connection is always considered the cosmic axis of the ritual.

Both Erzulie and Legba likewise have as their ritual attributes the
heart and the blood, which they control biologically. Most often it is
from among the singers that the mystères, magnetized in the atmosphere by the songs, choose their "mounts." Often a houn'sih is seen
to stagger, to whirl upon herself violently, throwing her arms out in
all directions in the classic gestures always made in an attempt to
ward off the mystère, and then to fall backwards upon the legs of the
seated spectators. Once the loa is finally in complete possession of her,
she quickly rises, and with a rush, dashes into the middle of the peristyle, her personality completely transformed. She then proceeds with
the customary activities of the mystère concerned.

Sometimes the loa who has thus mounted a houn'sih continues to
participate in the chorus, even though the possession has entirely ob-
literated the consciousness of the "horse." After the houn'sih has been
"dismounted," she simply resumes her place among the singers. It is
extremely rare, incidentally, ever to see a houn'guénicon overcome by
the loa-crisis.

Chants

Inconnection with our account of the chorus, the drums, the ogan,
the triangle, and the mode of chromatic communication with the
mystères of the invisible who dwell in the atmosphere, the ritual chants
—a clear expression of the sacred music—have significance and useful-
ness.

The repertory of Voodoo chants is so vast that it is impossible to say
how many there are—thousands, at least. They show variations, within
the same musical mode, from one region to another. For example, a
chant sung in one way at Port-au-Prince is sung in another at Port-de-
Paix. The chant is obviously the same and has come from the same
traditional, magical source, but with variations.

Every rite has its particular rhythm to which its chants are sung, although from one rite to another the difference in rhythm is not so great as to prevent one from realizing that, in any case, he is hearing Voodoo chants. Such is the difference, for example, between the Pethro and the Congo chants.

Accordingly, it is unnecessary to mention that the same phenomenon is observed in the music. The variations in the music correspond to the differences in the repertory of chants. Wherefore, however little a person is acquainted with Voodoo, as soon as he hears the music, he can tell whether it is from a Pethro or a Congo ceremony, a Pethro or a Congo dance, or a Rada or an Ibo service, as easily as he can distinguish the Congo from the Rada simply on the basis of the drum beats.

It happens in the course of a given ceremony that chants of different rites succeed and overlap one another because the mystères that appear are themselves different, or because more than one category of loas is being served.

It is useful to observe the double economy of every Voodoo chant. Not only may they belong to different rites—the Ibo, Congo, Rada, Pethro, Caplaou, Mahi, and others—but the sense of their words indicates the ritual and magical significance of their use in a particular ceremony. This means that if, for example, a certain chant asks Legba to "open the way" (speaking in magical terms), Legba is peremptorily charged with opening the way and not doing otherwise. If another chant alludes to Erzulie embarking upon the ocean, it refers either to her actual embarkation or to some very close allusion relating to the result sought by the cabalistic acts of the ceremony. Hence, the magical indications are made in accordance with the words sung.

Here are a few examples of Voodoo chants which mention some of the different rites:

Congo

Caroline saisie; cé loa moin.	Caroline is astonished; she's my loa.
Danbhalah Wédo,	Danbhalah Wédo,
m'a p' ba ou Bon Dié.	I will give you God.
M' cé Créole Congo,	I'm a Créole from the Congo,
m' pas sotto oh!	I'm no fool!
Danbhalah Wédo,	Danbhalah Wédo,

côté ou yé?	where are you?
Soleil-a lévé lan pays Congo!	The sun will rise in Congo-land!

Caplaou

Benga, manman moin!	Benga, my mother!
O, Zoclimo parlé,	O, Zoclimo speaks,
yo pas couté. Ouaille oh!	they don't listen. Ouai-oh!
Benga, manman,	Benga, mother,
si ou allé, pas tounin	if you leave, don't return
lan pays-a.	to this country.
Poussé allé, Zo, oui.	Go away, Zo, yes.
Poussé allé, kinbois salay,	Go away, kinbois salay,
Poussé allé, mi salay!	Go away, my salay!

Rada

O Legba! Commandé,	O Legba! Give orders,
Vié Legba! Commandé.	Old Legba! Give orders.
Commandé-yo.	Give them orders.

Ibo

Pagnin couvri pagnin,	Basket covers basket,
nanchon Ibo.	Ibo gods.
Pagnin couvri pagnin.	Basket covers basket.
Min pagnin, Grande Ibo,	Here's a basket, Grande Ibo,
Min pagnin.	Here's a basket.
Pagnin couvri pagnin,	Basket covers basket,
nanchon Ibo.	Ibo gods.

Anmine

Garde moin là. Tâté!
O! Garde moin là.
Tâté coffré!
Bo Ouanminan, Ouanminan,
con ça n'a p' blani yé.
Ouanminan, hé!
Garde moin chiré.

My talisman is there. Test it!
O! My talisman is there.
Test it, lock it up!
Bo Ouanminan, Ouanminan,
that's how we are serving.
Ouanminan, hey!
My talisman is torn.

Ibo-Mondongue

Eh! Roi Zan. Eh!
Roi Zan-Zan, Nanchon Ibo!
Hé, roi nanchon Ibo!
Vive, nanchon Ibo!
Côté Grande Ibo? Hé! Roi!
Hé! Roi Ibo mangé chien.

Eh! King Zan. Eh!
King Zan-Zan, Ibo gods!
Hey, King of the Ibo gods!
Hail, Ibo gods!
Where's Grande Ibo? Hey! King!
Hey! King Ibo eats dog.

Pethro

Ahi, manman, hen!
Tambour moin rélé.
Jou-m' allongé . . . Ahi!
Ahi! Manman.

Ahi, mother, hen!
My drum calls.
The day I die . . . Ahi!
Ahi! Mother.

Salengro

Trou Sa, Trou Sa,
Rélé trou Salengro.
N'a rélé trou Salengro.
Trou Sa, Trou Sa,
rélé trou Salengro!

That hole, That hole,
is called the Salengro hole.
We'll call the hole Salengro.
That hole, That hole,
called the Salengro hole!

Kitha-Zandor

Zan-dor! Li allé, Zan-dor!   Zandor! He's gone, Zandor!
Qui l'heù li yé? Zan-dor!   What time is it? Zandor!
Li allé, Zan-dor!   He's gone, Zandor!

Anmine-Makanda

Ouanminan! Ca ça yé,   Ouanminan! What's that,
Ouanminan? Tâté-coffré,   Ouanminan? Test it, lock it up,
Ca ça yé? A-Lah-Da dérivé.   What's that? A-Lah-Da is adrift.
Ca li yé, Ouanminan,   What is it, Ouanminan,
Garde O?   O Guard?

Because the chants mean exactly what their words clearly suggest, the chorus "sends" them, addresses them to the loas personally. As we shall see, these ritual chants which request the loas to do one thing or another are adapted to the rites in which the loas "work." For example:

Yanvalou

(chant for the mystère Manman Brigitte)

Manman Brigitte! Manman moin!   Mother Brigitte! My mother!
O! Ou ouè ça?   Oh! Do you see that?
À l'entour caille-là,   Around the house,
gangnin di fé là-dans ni.   there's a fire in it.
Nous chaché bois   We gather wood
pou nous semblé di fé;   to build a fire;
nous chaché d'l'eau pou nous   we gather water to
touyé di fé.   extinguish the fire.
La plus par tombé.   The rain does not fall.
Ou pas oué?   Don't you see?
Terre-là glissé.   The ground is slippery.

Yanvalou-Fla Vodoun
(chant for the mystère Jupiter-Québiésou)

Bagui-a lovi, mon roi!	The bagui's members, my king!
Cé ça, m'a ouè yo.	That's it—I shall see them.
Ahi! Manmouleh-vi.	Ahi! Manmouleh-vi.
Cé ça, Mahi Gouéto.	That's it, Mahi Gouéto.
Pò diable! Posso nou-deh.	Poor devil! Posso nou-deh.
Hé! An-hé!	Hey! An-hey!

Mahi
(chant for the mystère Mademoiselle Annaïse)

Annaïse! En Nago,	Annaïse! En Nago,
pitite-là apé crié.	the baby is crying.
Yé, yé! Ba-li tété. Yé, yé!	Yey, yey! Give him a teat. Yey, yey!
Apé crié, yé, yé!	He's crying, yey, yey!
Ba-li tété, Ba-li tete, yé, yé!	Give him a teat, yey, yey!
Gadé: m'lan bâton. Yé, yé!	Look: I'm benrenek. Yey, yey!
Ba-li tété, yé, yé!	Give him a teat, yey, yey!

Martinique
(chant for the mystère Nan Kiou)

Cousin Nan-Kiou,	Cousin Nan-Kiou,
cé pa ça ou té dit moin.	that's not what you told me.
Ou té dit moin con ça:	You told me:
Jou oua plaçé avè m'	"the day you become my mistress
oua marié avè m'.	you would marry me."
Nan point robe, nan point chemise.	I haven't a dress, not even a shirt.
Grand merci gnou pied mango qui te gaign en ba-à qui paré l'honneur moin.	There's only a mango tree that I had there to bolster my reputation.

Crabigne Nago
(chant for the mystère Ogou Shalodeh)

Liki, liki ô! Liki, liki ô!   Liki, liki Oh! Liki, liki Oh!
Ogou Shalodeh.   Ogou Shalodeh.
Papa Ogou Jacouman,   Papa Ogou Jacouman,
Papa Ogou Shalodeh.   Papa Ogou Shalodeh.
Liki, liki ô! Liki, liki ô!   Liki, liki Oh! Liki, liki Oh!
Ogou Shalodeh.   Ogou Shalodeh.

Congo
(chant for the mystère Legba)

Legba lan oum'phor moin!   Legba in my oum'phor!
Legba lan oum'phor moin!   Legba in my oum'phor!
Ou minme qui pôté chapeau.   You who wear a hat.
Cé pou paré soleil pou moin.   It is to protect me from the sun.
Legba Congo nan oum'phor moin,   Legba Congo in my oum'phor,
Mondongue-Moussai lan   Mondongue-Moussai in
oum'phor moin.   my oum'phor.

To show more clearly by a convincing synthesis the astral relationships existing among the rites, the mystères, and the chants "sent" to the chorus of houn'sih canzos by either the houn'guénicon or the houn'gan during the course of a *service-loa*, the following examples are given of a few of the chants classified according to the rites in which they are performed:

Yanvalou
(chant for Legba, loa of gates and roads)

Legba-Grand-Chemin, nous   Legba-Highway, we are going.
   pr'allé.

Ago, Ago yé.	Ago, Ago yey.
Legba-Grand-Chemin, nous pr'allé	Legba-Highway, we are going
ouè si n'a passé;	to see if we shall pass;
Legba-Grand-Chemin, nous pr'allé	Legba-Highway, we are going
ouè, Papa, si n'a passé.	to see, Papa, if we shall pass.
Si n'a passé grand-chemin,	If we shall pass the highway,
mon roi!	my king!
Ago! Grand-Chemin, nous pr'allé	Ago! Highway, we are going
ouè, Papa, si n'a passé.	to see, Papa, if we shall pass.
O Ago! Ago yé!	Oh Ago! Ago yey.

Yanvalou

(chant for Danbhalah and Aï-Da Wédo)

Danbhalah Wédo,	Danbhalah Wédo,
gadé pitites ou yo, hé!	behold your children, hey!
Aïda Wédo, min pitites ou yo,	Aïda Wédo, here are your children,
hé!	hey!
Danbhalah Wédo,	Danbhalah Wédo,
gadé pitites ou yo, oh!	behold your children, oh!
A yé, a yé, oh!	A yey, a yey, oh!
Danbhalah, min z'enfants ou là.	Danbhalah, here are your children.

Nago

(chant for Aloumandia, one of the *maître-tête* mystères of Dessalines; Aloumandia is here associated with the mystères Ossangne Bacoulé and Ogou Badagri)

Alou Madia hé! Ossangne oh!	Alou Madia hey! Ossangne oh!
Ogou oh!	Ogou oh!
Ossangne Bacoulé qui mandé	Ossangne Bacoulé who asks for
drapeaux.	flags.
Alou Madia hé! Ossangne oh!	Alou Madia hey! Ossangne oh!

Ogou oh!	Ogou oh!
Ogou Badagri qui mandé	Ogou Badagri who asks for
drapeaux,	flags,
Nous tout barré.	We are all barred.

Mahi

(chant for Erzulie Fréda)

Cé chance oh! O, cé chance oh!	It's luck, oh! O, it's luck, oh!
Cé pas wanga ou gangnin;	It's not a magic charm that you
	have;
cé chance oh!	it's luck, oh!
Grande Erzulie Fréda,	Grande Erzulie Fréda,
cé chance ou gangnin.	it's luck that you have.
Cé pas wanga ou gangnin;	it's not a magic charm that you
	have;
cé chance, O Maîtresse.	it's luck, O Mistress.

Congo - Crabigne

(chant for Moussondi, or for a Moussongui loa)

Hé ya hé! Hé ya Moussondi!	Hey yah hey! Hey yah Moussondi!
Loa cila-à, cé loa Moussondi.	That loa—that's the Moussondi loa.
Hé ya hé! Hé ya Moussondi!	Hey yah hey! Hey yah Moussondi!

Kitha

(degree-chant composed by the mystère Brisé)

L'ennemi barré moin	The enemy stops me
caille Santo.	at Santo's house.
M' passé déjà.	I already passed.
Zombi barré moin	A zombi bars me

caille Santo	at Santo's house.
Caille Santo, m'passé déjà!	At Santo's house I already passed!

Banda
(chant for Guédé Nibbho, Lord of the Cemeteries)

Hé! Gros saint, gros loa,	Hey! Great saint, great loa,
Guédé Nibbho égaré!	Guédé Nibbho is lost!
Hé! Gros saint, gros loa,	Hey! Great saint, great loa,
Papa Guédé égaré.	Papa Guédé is lost.

Pethro (Banda - - - Crabigne)
(chant for the loa Jean Zombi)

Jean Zombi! Oui-oua, ba!	Jean Zombi! Oui-oua, bah!
Conduis-m' allé.	Take me away.
Ya p'boué tafia pou yo fait	They will drink tafia to make them
tintin	grimace
devant loa moin.	before my loa.
Jean Zombi! Oui-oua, ba!	Jean Zombi! Oui-oua, bah!
Conduis-m' allé.	Take me away.

Ibo
(chant for the mystère Ayanman)

Ayanman! Ibo Lélé, Lélé, Lélé!	Ayanman! Ibo Lélé, Lélé, Lélé!
Ayanman! Ibo Lélé!	Ayanman! Ibo Lélé!
Ayanman ça, con ça;	Ayanman, that's the way, like that;
Ayanman dansé con ça.	Ayanman dances like that.
Ou pilé pied-m',	You step on my foot,
ou pas di-m' "padon."	you don't say "pardon."
Ayanman ça, con ça;	Ayanman, that way, like that;
Ayanman ça, con ça;	Ayanman, that way, like that;
ça "padon" t'a fait pou moin?	What would a "pardon" do for me?

Caplaou
(chant for the mystère Zo Climo)

Zo! Comment ça yé?	Zo! How's that?
Zo Benga, Papa! Comment ça yé?	Zo Benga, Papa! How's that?
Zo Climan, Papa, comment ça yé?	Zo Climan, Papa, how's that?
Si houn'sih tombé,	If the houn'sih falls,
pas quitté-l' gâté	don't let her spoil (things)
avant yo fouillé trou.	before they dig a hole.

Although this classification shows the rites to which certain mystères belong, it does not imply that they belong exclusively to any one rite. Hence, if an initiate wishes to "serve" a Rada Legba in the Pethro rite, it is perfectly possible to do so. But according to some initiates it is only the *loa-Guinin* (the purest African loas) who refuse to be served on any "point" (that is, in any rite) except their own. Plausible as this assertion may seem, however, the proof to the contrary lies in the fact that most of the loas are found in most of the rites. The purpose which requires the serving of loas first on one "point" and then on another depends upon the form of magic in question, that is, whether the mystères are being invoked with good or evil intent.

When Voodoo reached Hispaniola with the first slaves purchased on the Atlantic coasts of Africa, its ritual chants were in the pure African *langage*, a synthesis of all the African dialects which form the "Great Magic Language" of the tradition. Nevertheless, each rite, or each "nation" of loas has preserved its own langage: Nago, Congo, Pethro, Anmine, and the others. Thus in the vast repertory of Voodoo chants are found those which belong to many different African dialects.

The relations of the slaves with the English, Spanish, and French colonists resulted in the creation of a mixed language which was to become the Creole spoken in Haiti today, an extremely rich and supple language composed of all that the African had been able to retain not only of the hundreds of African dialects, but of French, English, and Spanish. Thus the greatest part of the chants of the ritual repertory of Voodoo have evolved from the pure African language to Creole. Occasionally Creole, French, and African are mingled to make a single chant. Other times the chant is one hundred percent Creole. Furthermore, certain chants have remained absolutely African. These are said to be in *langage*. These for the most part have been retained in a mnemonic tradition, but very few houn'gans or houn'sihs are able any longer to translate them. They somehow "feel" atavistically what they mean. The disturbing result of this transformation, in which the chants in *langage* are unfortunately disappearing more and more, is that the purity of the Voodoo cabal as well as the very power of the loas is being lost at the same time and in the same proportion. It is also to be regretted that the chants in mixed language or purely Creole lack the liturgical poetry of the chants in *langage*, which gives an air so mysterious and at the same time so effective in the ceremonies. Here are some examples:

A Voodoo Chant in Pure Haitian Creole
(Ancient Yanvalou Ritual)

N'a rémècié, n'a rémècié yo . . .	We will thank, we will thank them . . .
Apré Bon Dié, n'a rémècié yo.	After God we will thank them.
Apré Bon Dié, nous là;	After God, we are there;
n'a rémècié yo;	we will thank them;
N'a rémècii Dié douvant houn'gan	We will thank God before the houn'gan . . .
N'a rémèci d'l'eau dòmi houn'gan . . .	We will thank the water ? houn'gan . . .
N'a rémèci, n'a rémècié yo.	We will thank, we will thank them.
N'a rémècié houn'guénicon,	We will thank the houn'guénicon,
N'a rémèci houn'sih canzo . . .	We will thank the houn'sih canzo . . .

(Voodoo Chant: Mixed Creole, French, and *langage*) (Caplaou)

Benga, manman moin . . .O, Zoclimo!	Benga, my mother . . . O, Zoclimo!
Ou pâlé, yo pas couté. Oua yo!	You speak, they don't listen. Oua yo!
Benga, manman, si ou allé,	Benga, mother. If you go,
ou pas tounin lan pays-à.	you do not return to the country.
Poussez aller, Zo oui . . .	Hurry and go, Zo oui . . .
Poussez aller, kim'boi salay,	Hurry and go, kim'boi salay,
Poussez aller, mi saloy	Hurry and go, mi saloy.

(Voodoo Chant in Pure *langage*) (Yanvalou)

Minoké ago Legba. Ago Legba, ago Legba!
Go Legba, Go Legba.
Minoké ago Legba . . . .

(Another Voodoo Chant in Pure *langage*) (Yanvalou)

Zouzou zouzou zi za, i mankou tuilé.
Bléo, bléo . . .
Marasah-Guinin, a i mankou tuilé;
Bléo, bléo . . .
I mankou tuilé, Marssah-Guinin;
Bléo, bléo . . .

We choose now a certain Voodoo text relative to the Nago loas of
Yoruba, translating it into French to show the phonetic divergence
which results from the translation from one language to another. The
translation into Creole follows the French translation to clarify this
divergence and to show how the African *voudouns* can be distorted.
This is a Yoruba chant for the mystère A Gbo Gbo, recognized today
in the Voodoo practiced in Haiti in the expression "Abobo!" It is a
mystère who interrupts the chants and who exalts the Invisibles in its
double signification of "Alleluia!"

—Olih kolo mon deh, Abobo!

—A wa na?
—N'wa é, Abobo . . .
Abobo fo laga jigi légan.

—Ikou kati, ko ka mi . . .
I hou mi kpon, é ma gnon
O lou ièbé, Ifé,
To é mé médeh ma non yi ré
Lobi Olo-run.

Translation into Creole:

—C'é moin qui pôté cècueil,
    Abobo!
—Ah! C'é ou minme?

Je suis le porteur de cercueil,
    Abobo!
Ah! Ah; C'est toi?
C'est bien moi, Abobo . . .
Je couple l'air (le chant) avec
    authorité.
Garde-moi de la mort insatiable . . .
Me tuer serait un crime,
Car le Grand Roi d'Ifé,
Le pays où ne vont pas les vivants,
A créé la Lumière.

Translation into English:

I am the bearer of the coffin,
    Abobo!
Ah! Is it you?

—Oui, c'é moin, Abobo!   Yes, it is I, Abobo!
M'gain pouvoi pou m'rété chantés.   I have the power to "cut" the chant.
—Empéchez lan-mò prend-m',   Take (me), keep me from death,
Pace que si ou tuez-m' c'é   For if you kill me, it's
  gnou crime,   a crime,
Pisqué c'é Grand Roi d'Ifé,   Since it is the Great King of Ifé,
Côté mòtels pas janme allé,   Where mortals never go,
Qui ban nous limiè.   Who gives us the light (i.e., of life).

The symbol of the solar ravishment is the sword or machete of the Voodoo ritual. The following is a ritual chant to bring about the arrest by the police of anyone who steals this symbol:

Kadia Bossou, Yahiwé (Ié-H-Wé),   Kadia Bossou, Yawé,
Yahwé, Yahwé, Ya Bossou,   Yahwé, Yahwé, Ya Bossou,
A Dié, Yahwé mrin, Bossou mrin!   Ah God, my Yahwé, my Bossou!
A Dié; couline ça-a, cé pou   Ah God; that machette, it's for
  Yahwé . . .   Yahwé . . .
Cé pou Yahwé-Aida   It's for Yahwé-Aida
Yahwé, Yahwé!   Yahwé, Yahwé!
Cé la police, O ya lagué la police   It's the police, Oh, they will call
  'lan cò-ou.   the police against you.
Cé pou Yahwé Camblanmin.   It's for Yahwé Camblanmin.

Voodoo Dances

In the preceding section the explanation of the performance of ritual chants in accordance with particular rites is sufficient to show that the rites, by the evidence of their names alone, are related to the musical repertory. The relationships between the liturgy and the choreography established in Voodoo by this fact clearly indicate the cabalistic function of the dances and reveal their relation to the legislative and governmental system of the astral upon which the cult of the loas is based.

All the chant rhythms based upon corresponding musical themes that mention both the ritual behavior and the *nations, tribes,* or *races* of the loas have been preserved in Haitian Voodoo exactly as the slaves brought them to Haiti in the old days from the Ivory Coast, the

Gold Coast, the Grain Coast, from Senegal, Angola, the Congo, Dahomey, Yoruba, Sudan, and elsewhere. Furthermore, the identification of the rites by the names of still existing African tribes clearly proves their origin.

It remains to be noted that while the chants of the various rites differ from one another, there is comparatively far greater difference between the dances. For example, an *Ibo dance* differs more from a *Mahi dance* than an *Ibo chant* from a *Mahi chant*. However, perhaps this judgement is based upon the illusion that the sense of sight is more immediately sensitive to movement than the sense of hearing is to the metaphysics of music.

Nevertheless, as a rule the names of the chants and the dances classed according to rites or to *nations* should automatically indicate the composition of the batteries of drums as well as the manner in which the drums are played. The following list is a modest attempt to classify both the dances and the fundamental rites that are performed in Haitian oum'phors today, omitting those of secondary importance.

Rada (3 drums)

> Voodoo dance
> Fla voudoun

Pethro (2 drums)

> Kitha
> Kitha mouillé (wet Kitha)
> Kitha sec (dry Kitha)

Congo (2 or 3 drums)

> Congo paillettes
> Congo mazonne
> Congo Créole
> Congo Franc

Congo Guinée
Congo Larose
Congo-Pethro

Ibo (3 drums)

Mabi (3 drums)

Nago (3 drums)

Dahomée (3 drums)

Dahomée z'épaules
Djouba Franc
Djouba Martinique
Djouba Baboule
Moussongui
Boum'ba-Lem'ba (Pethro)
Salengro (Congo-Guinée)
Caplaou-Canga

Asson-Rou (Yan-Valou) (3 drums)

Yanvalou Franc
Yanvalou cassé
Yanvalou Nago
Yanvalou z'épaules
Yanvalou genoux
Yanvalou debout
Yanvalou dos bas

Banda (3 drums)

Crabignin, Nago, Congo (3 drums)

The following dances and rites are also basically of African origin. They were found during the slave period and for some years after, but since that time have gradually disappeared:

Kitha (still seen today, but as part of the Pethro rite to which it does not properly belong)
Caplaou
Caplaou-Canga
Salengro

The following dances and rites likewise bear names of historical and geographical significance, but are combined in one way or another with the first fundamental group—the Rada—which, moreover, influences voodoo choreography:

Fon
Mandingue
Moundongue
Foulah
Soco-lo
Bambara
Haoussah
Mayombeh
Sobo-houn
Mascotte
Congo-Guinin-houn'tò-Gouétò
Makandal

There are also other secondary dances that can be mentioned, and which are variously related to the fundamental group. However, the exact relationship between them and the fundamental group is never very precise or formal. These are the:

Carabienne

Pastorelle
Mout-séché
Bouleverse

The two great dances of totally popular character whose origin is found in the African mask rituals should not be omitted:

Mascaron (of the Pethro rite)
Méringue (of mixed rite: Pethro-Rada)

Because of their very origin, these have became the official dances of the two greatest carnival masked bands in Haiti, likewise called the Mascaron and the Méringue.

Last of all, there is another popular dance—the Rara—performed to an orchestral accompaniment dominated by *vaccines*, or bamboo flutes. It is of Voodoo origin, and is usually danced along country roads. It "walks" upon very powerful "points" in magic, because of the instrument used by the "king" or "ra" of these bands: a staff decorated with tin ornaments, with which he does all sorts of marvellous things. Naturally, this staff corresponds to the staff of Legba, for good intent or for evil.

The most important thing to remember about all the Voodoo dances is that, just like all the other factors of the cult, they correspond to elements of the astral which the study of African esoterism attempts to clarify. Like the chants, the *vèvès* or ritual diagrams, and the drums, they are capable of initiating communication with the forces of the invisible, for they represent choreographically the very forces that they reproduce.

Voodoo Prayers

Voodoo ceremonies always commence with prayers. These prayers are generally quite long, almost interminable. For this reason we shall demonstrate only their principle, with a view to showing the procedure employed by the houn'gan or the mam'bo, with the congregation giving the responses. These prayers are recited as litanies, as moving as they are soporific. They begin with the *Prière Guinin* (African Prayer), which demonstrates the religious syncretism operating between Africa and Rome; for this *Prière Guinin* is found to be a prayer said only in French, but including the names of Roman Catholic saints. The *Prière Djor*, or *Prière Dio*, follows in Voodoo "language," but mixed with French expressions and the names of saints of the Roman calendar.

The Catholic prayer and the *dior* prayer have as their special purpose the "preparing of the astral" in order to facilitate the ceremonial magic. They place the astral at the disposition of the houn'gan or the mam'bo. Also, these prayers are sung or followed by chants because the ritual chant is psycho-astral: it totalizes the causal spirit which presides over a religious or lay assembly for a greater control of the supernatural presences which are operating. They are these presences which voodooists call *vodoun, loa, voudoun,* or *mystères, anges* or *saints.*

When saying these prayers the houn'gan is usually seated before the centerpost (sometimes before the *pé*), on a low chair, asson and bell in hand with which he accents certain parts of this "spoken chant" comprising the *Prière Guinin* and the *Prière Djor*.

The leit-motif, "Lih-sah Do-lé, Zo . . ." which follows the catagories of mystères mentioned, shows that the prayer is placed under the influence of Legba, the old and wise, who represents thunder under the name of Québié-sou or Hé-Vio-Zo (the Québiésou Dan Leh of the Haitian oum'phor, supreme guardian of the purity of the Voodoo Tradition, and who personifies the "serpent of thunder."

The tradition of this prayer allows a charitable and deferential thought for the poor deceased, for the brother masons, for drums no longer used, for the former drummers, for all the old sacred musical instruments no longer usable or lost, for all cult objects broken or thrown away, and even for everything else that may have been forgotten.

Thus, in addition to being a great act of magic incantation having the religious power of concentrating all the traditional *psyche* of the deceased of the great universal tradition of religion, of which the houn'gan is about to serve as minister, the Voodoo prayer is a fantastic thank offering, and an immense tradition of charity. It embraces the three theological virtues upon which the African cabal is based from its origin: Faith, Hope, and Charity.

This is the form of the Roman Catholic Prayer, often recited by a

père savane, or "bush priest," that is, by an acolyte or sacristan of the
Roman Church paid by the oum'phor—a paradox inasmuch as Rome is
fiercely opposed to Voodoo.

Our Father . . .
Hail Mary . . .
Creed . . .
Glory be to the Father . . .
Hail Mary, hear my prayers . . .
Holy Angels, we are on our knees at the feet of Mary . . .
Saint Rose, hear us . . .
Jesus, hear us . . .
Saint Peter, give us the key which opens the gate . . .
Great saints, give us our powers . . .
Saint Anthony, hear us . . .
Come, my God, Come . . .
The angel of the Lord said to Mary that she was pregnant with
    Jesus Christ . . .
Saint Philomena, virgin and martyr . . .
Holy virgins, hear us . . .
Alas, Alas, Mary Magdalene . . .
Oh, Lord Jesus in the Host . . .
Grace, Mary, grace . . .
In the name of the Father, the Son, and the Holy Ghost . . .
We hail Thee, O Mary, hear our prayers, and place us in heaven
    to serve you . . .
Great God, intercede for us . . .
Saint Joseph, intercede with Jesus, our Redeemer, for us . . .
Saint Joseph, charm, charm our eyes . . .
Angel of heaven, have pity on us . . .
Saint Andrew and Holy Angels, behold us at your knees at the
    feet of Mary . . .
All saints, all saints, all saints, hear us . . .
Saint Anthony of Padua, hear us . . .
Saint James, hear us . . .
Saint Philipp, hear us . . .
Saint John the Baptist, hear us . . .

—other invocations follow.

This is the form of the *Prière Djor:*

(1) Litany of the *Djor* saints, a vast syncretism of the oum'phor and Rome:

Rhélez (or *helez,* or *appelez* = "call," "summon," "hail") The Great Eternal Father, The Djor Saints, Oh! Hail The Great Eternal Father, the Saints Djor Docoi Agoueh. Hail The Great Eternal Father, if we are in the hands of Bon Dieu (The Good God), Oh Saints . . .
Apo Lihsah G Bhadia Wangan Ciétò Lihsah Doleh Zo!
Hail the Virgin Mary . . .
Hail the Virgin of Good Help . . .
Hail the Master Creator of heaven and of earth . . .
Hail Saint Anthony of Padua . . .
Hail Saint Nicholas . . .
Hail Holy Ghost . . .
. . . . Lihsah Doleh Zo!
Hail Saint Andrew . . .
Hail Saint Joseph . . .
Hail Saint Moses . . .

The following saints are invoked as above: Saints Augustine, Savior, Gerard, Ulrich, Patrick (Danbhalah Wédo), Comas and Damien (the Mara-sah), John, Luke, Mark, Matthiew, Peter, Paul, James, Philipp, Charles Borromeo, Virgin of the Rosary, Virgin of Mercy, Great Saint Ann (Dèla-i-e Médeh), the Immaculate Conception, the Virgin Altagrâce, the Virgin of Charity, the Virgin of Mount Carmel, Saint Clare, Philomena, Alberic, and all the male and female saints in heaven. Occasionally these invocations are interrupted with the cry, "Lihsah Doleh Zo!

(2) Litany of *Djor* mystères, the purely African loas:

Hail Mara-sah, Djor saints, é, Docoi Agoueh, if we are in the hands of the
Bon Dieu (the Good God), Oh Saints . . .
Hail Legba Ait-Bon, Djor é . . .
Hail Ai-Zan Vélé-Kétheh . . .

The formula repeated, invoking the following loas: Loco Ati-sou Poun'goué, Marasahs: Do-sou, Do-sah, Do-goueh, Do-i-chou, Do-can, Bois. Hail Danbhalah and Aida Wédo, Lihsah Doleh Zo! Hail Sobo Kè-sou, Badè-sih Croix-la-hounsih, Aga-sou Yinmin, Silibo Vavou, Agoueh Ta R Oyo, Maître Agoueh R Oyo, Erzulie Fréda Tocan Miroi-Zan Zangaza, Maîtresse La Sirène, Maîtresse La Balein, Bo-sou Canblanmin, Agaou Tonnerre, Azaca Médeh, Bélécou Yenou, Ogou Badagri, Ogou Ferraille, Ogou Bhathalah, Ogou Chango, Baco-sou Aladeh, Adoum' Guidi, Ogou Ashadeh (an ancient Dahomean king), Ogou Bhalin'dio, Ogou Palama, Ossange Mégui Malor, Lingle-sou, Grande Bossine, Grande Avélé-Kétheh, Mambo Nanan, Grande Tèsih Fréda, Grande Dan-i (a very old serpent of the Tradition), Grande Alouba, Grande Aloumandia, é, Baron Samedi, Guédé Nouvavou, Brutus Jean-Simon, Simbi Yandé-Zo Yan-kitha, Yam-Polah, Toutou Houn'gan, Toutou Mambo, Toutou Houn'guénicon, Toutou Houn'sih Can-Zo, Toutou La Place Guinin, Toutou Porte-Drapeau Guinin, Toutou Houn'tò-qui (the drummers), Toutou Ogantieh (the ogan player), Toutou Houn'sih dé-sou-nin, Toutou l'Afrique Guinin. Zo! Lihsah Doleh Zo! Hail all Mambos, Hail all Houn'gans. The following "nations" of loas are invoked: Rada, Pethro, Ibo, Caplaou, An-mine, Ti-Brutus, Mondongue, Mandingue, Sinigal, Canga-Leh, Kitha, Kitha-sè, Kitha mouillé, Congo, Nago, Nago Iki, Ibi-Lihki, Dan-homeh, Zo! Lihsah Doleh Zo!

The choir of houn'sihs kiss the ground while kneeling, and sing, "Miguel . . . Oh, Magnofoueh!!! (Note: this ritual of general invocation varys linguistically according as it is observed by the Congos, the Ibos, the Pethros, the Radas, the Anmines, or the Nagos).

We have presented one of the traditional forms of the prayers because in our own experience it is difficult if not impossible to indicate any invariable method of reciting the prayers and singing the ritual chants of Voodoo at the commencement of a religious service. The result is that if the tradition itself were fixed, definite, and unchangable, the different Voodoo societies would in any case progressively alter purely traditional prayers and chants, ending up with their own versions of prayers and chants. Thus, even though all the prayers and chants are basically similar, they differ so much that the houn'sih choir of one oum'phor is not necessarily able to give the responses to prayers and chants "sent" by the houn'gan or houn'guénicon of another oum'phor. This is frequently observed because the houn'gans and mam'bos of different oum'phors frequently are visitors and lend their aid in maintaining the tradition in other oum'phors. For example, if a houn'guénicon of Port-de-Paix, in northwest Haiti, "sends" the chants in an oum'phor of Crois-des-Missions, in western Haiti, the choir of the oum'phor at Croix-des-Missions may have great difficulty in giving the response.

Nevertheless, to give a more or less definite idea of the manner of reciting these prayers and performing these chants of the voodoo ritual, we have taken the pains to record carefully the regular succession of some of them as is practiced in an oum'phor at Croix-des-Missions. This order of prayers applies to a Voodoo service in the Pethro rite:

PRAYERS:
  (1) Roman Catholic Prayers:
      Our Father   (
      Hail Mary   (1) French
      Creed   (2) Latin
      Confiteor   (

SONGS: (French)
  (2) The angel of the Lord said to Mary that she would conceive of the Holy Ghost
      Come, My God, Come
      Grâce, Mary, Grâce . . .

      (In Creole)

      Holy Mary, Mother of God, pray for the Saints . . .
      Danbhalah-Wédo, assuage your children . . .
      Danbhalah-Wédo, we are all angels . . .

LITANY OF THE VOUDOUN:
  (3) (Note: After each invocation the houn'sihs respond: *cé z'anges!*)
      Diabolo Bo-sou . . . .   cé z'anges
      Agaou Tonnerre . . . .   "

Sim'bi An-Dé-Zo . . .	cé z'anges
Loumandia . . .	"
Kitha Malor . . .	"
Azagon . . .	"
Houn'gan Saloperie . . .	"
Houn'gan paternels . . .	"
Houn'gan maternels . . .	"

(leit-motif pronounced by the houn'gan):

Danbhalah-Wédo!	We are all angels, Oh, Oh, Oh!
Ogou Bhathalah . . .	"
Ogou Chango . . .	"
Adoum' Guidi . . .	"
Danbhalah-Wédo!	"

VOODOO SONGS (in *langage*, sometimes mixed with Creole):
(4) Toni rhélé Congo . . .
   O, Sim'bi, anhé! Manman-mrin, O Iké Mam'bré . . .
   Moin dit ou, gangan yo . . . ("I tell you, the houn'gans")
   O, Ouanguileh, kim'boi sala . . .
   O, Wangol, O, ou a montré-m' la priè qui minnin Africains
      sòti lan Guinin: trois paters, trois avé Marias . . .
   An, an! Madioman, an, an . . .

LITANY OF THE VOUDOUN:

                                              Response
(5) Calfou Boum'ba . . .   An, an! Madioman, an, an, . . .
   Toutes loa Kitha . . . (All Kitha loas)   "
   Toutes houn'sih dans le ciel . . .   "
   Kitha Maza . . .   "
   Poun'goueh Gangan . . .   "
   Zila Congo . . .   "
   Moussai . . .   "

VOODOO CHANTS (in Creole and in *langage*):
(6) Janmin, janmin, Ti Kitha Poun'goueh . . .
   O, salue moin! Gangan moin, Bacaya Ba-Ka . . .
The same chants continue to accompany the rest of the ceremony:

	Response
Sophie Congo . . .	Baka-Lah, an-hé ô, Baka-Lah!
Houn'gan Maternel . . .	"
Houn'gan Paternel . . .	"
Québié-sou . . .	"
Sim'bi Y-an-Kitha . . .	"
Zilah Mo-yo . . .	"
Kitha Malor . . .	"
Jean-Pierre Poungoueh . . .	"

These invocations and responses may continue indefinitely. The fundamental principle of Voodoo is clearly observed in the chant "O, Wangol, Ô, ou a montré-m' la priè qui minnin Africains sòti lan Guinin: trois Pater, trois Ave Maria" ("Oh Wangol, Oh! You have shown me the prayer which leads Africans out of Guinea, [Africa]: [Say] three Our Fathers, three Ave Marias.") which refers to the voyage of initiation in Africa, to Ifé or Ilé. This principle above all must be remembered in order to understand Voodoo. Ifé or Ilé (*lan z'ilets*, as Haitians say) is therefore the Promised Land: the land which necessarily is found on the other side of the water, and which the Tradition translates as follows:

Ifé, or Ilé: The Land
Olo, or Oro: Promise

6

Performing Voodoo Magic

W ITH the previous chapters as a background, the reader needs
only to know something of the procedural method in order to attempt
to perform a Voodoo ceremony. The instructions that follow are con-
densed as much as possible because the writer believes that in Voodoo
magic, as in every other kind of magic, there are fewer requirements
for success than most people generally imagine. Most important is a
good understanding of the principles.

In the foregoing synthesis—a true summary of the principles of
magic—the writer has not been content merely to gather information
from Haitian Voodoo practitioners and from his own observations,
but he has diligently gone back to the African sources of Voodoo that
have been somewhat altered by the Créole of the West Indies. Compared with Haitian practices, the truly African procedural method in
Voodoo is purer, simpler, and more efficacious, without the useless
accumulations which have grown out of individual preferences or are
the result of a lack of initiative preparation verging on heterodoxy.
The writer's intention has been encouraged by numerous houn'gans
who, having steeped themselves in the authentic sources of Voodoo,
claim that they "work" with an *asson-Guinin* (an "African asson").

The *Tradition-Guinin,* or African tradition, teaches one thing that the practitioner should not lose sight of when performing a ceremony: the phenomenal designs employed in magic are a simple modification of the "astral fluid of the earth." For this reason the magic signs—the vévés—are usually traced on the ground. These designs remain in the place to which the "firmly spoken will" of the celebrant "sends" them. This "astral fluid of the earth" is the "great magical agent" of Voodoo. It is expressed by the vèvès, which the loas of this supernatural agency immediately comprehend, to which they yield, and which they obey.

Procedures To Follow

Houn'gan crosses himself; he recites (or may omit) the *prière dior;* (1) With flour which has been oriented in the manner described below, he traces a vèvè, or synthetizing magic diagram.

The tracing is made upon the ground or upon a sheet of white paper which the celebrant places on a table. He then blows the remainder of the flour from the palm of his hand towards the four cardinal points.

The celebrant crosses himself thus:

on the forehead, or East, saying *Linsah;*

on the breast, or West, saying *Mawu;*

on the left shoulder, or North, saying *Vovo-Lin-V-Hwé*
                                      (Sakpata = Impurity)

on the right shoulder, or South, saying *Hévio-Zo*
(Ku-Ji = Purity)
He makes the sign of the cross over the ground:
(2) He says in a clear voice, loudly and with determination, three
times for each Spirit:
By the powers of Grand Maître: ATEGBINIMONSE ODAN-
BHALAH WEDO DANGBE TAU-CAN ZO A-GLA YE-WE,
By the powers of AIDA WEDO,
By the powers of TSILLAH WEDO,
By the powers of LOA-CAN LIH-CAN LEGBA ATI-BON, to
whom I say "Ké, Ecu-Mâlé, Gba, ké dounou nou Al Pha. Vou-
doun Yéké, hen-mi ace."
The celebrant orients a candle and some matches; he lights the
candle and places it on the table or inside the circle.
He orients the water in the same manner, namely East, West, North,
South.

(3) The celebrant calls out the name of each of the loas of the Ter-
restrial Fluid three times, and at each name throws three drops of
water on the ground in the form of a triangle:
By the powers of LEGBA ATIBON CATA-ROULO,
By the powers of GBA ADU,
By the powers of SEGBO LIHSAH,
By the powers of LOKO ATI-ZO,
By the powers of AI-ZAN A VELEH KETHEH,
By the powers of KEVIOZO DAN LEH,
By the powers of SIM'BHI IAN-DE-ZO IAN-PHA-CAN IAN-
KITHA,
By the powers of MAITRE AGOUEH RO IO,
By the powers of MAITRESSE ASE-I-LIH FRE-DA DAN-
HOME TAU-CAN MIROI-ZE ZAGAZA DAN-THOR ZAN-

DOR KITHA-SEC IBO CONGO CAPLAOU PETHRO NAGO
FON FOULAH RADA NAGO,
By the powers of DAN WU-E-ZO,
By the powers of OGOU FER,
By the powers of OGOU BHALIN'DIO,
By the powers of OGOU BHATHALAH,
By the powers of OGOU BHADAGRI,
By the powers of Grande FLEURIZON (FLEURI ZO),
By the powers of BOHO-VI (The Twins),
By the powers of Docteur PIQURES,
By the powers of LEM'BHA ZA-WU,
By the powers of ALOUMANDIA,
By the powers of all the Voudoun,
By the powers of FAITH, HOPE, AND CHARITY.

(4) The celebrant places or plants a golden pin (which has been oriented as above) upon or in the table, the stone of the socle, or within the circle of operation. To the pin he attaches a gold or silver chain (likewise oriented).

He sprinkles water upon the area of operation in a triangular pattern saying:

                                        BOLOU

                                        △

                            BOYE   BOCICE

In this way the Earth, as the Astral Light, thus nourished, may forge the magic chain which will produce the supernatural phenomenon. The earth then reacts by liberating the alchemic volatile in order to achieve the results dictated by the will of the celebrant.

The celebrant then announces what he desires the loas to do, terminating with the following potent formula:

KU DYO,
ATEGBINIMONSE,
LEGBA,
AGOO DI PHA HWE.

The following formula may be substituted for the preceding:

SILOE
AEI-LIH
AEI-LIH
AEI-LIH

LAMMA
SAH-BHA-K-THA-NI (to establish the fluid
circuit of the transubstantiation of power)
(5) He assists in the liberation of the "volatile" by spraying out of
his mouth the water which he has taken in three draughts, in order
to put into operation the transubstantiation of the sacramental material.

He sprinkles with perfume all the ceremonial facilities in order to
aid still further the transmission of the powers.

He dispatches the loas with these words:

YE-KE	=	The ensemble of the loas
MAR-CH-ALLAH!	=	"Peace be with you!"
KU M BHA-LAH DYA	=	"Withdraw into the Light."

Magic Baths of Voodoo

Voodoo practitioners have always attached considerable importance
to the "magic baths"—baths which they take in the oum'phor, in the
ocean, or at home, and about the composition of which they are very
much concerned. Peasants are not the only ones familiar with the
practice of ceremonial bathing. It is common knowledge that the
practice extends to people at the highest social levels. Haitian con-
gressional candidates and even candidates for the presidency are
known to have taken "magic baths" to improve their chances of being
elected.

One well known bath is the "Christmas Bath." Another is the "New
Year's Day Bath." In great numbers bathers wade into the ocean a
short distance from the shore carrying seven, ten, or twenty-one pieces
of a lime. As they dive in they pray the loas of the sea to prevent any
supernatural operations directed against them from touching them.
Agoueh R Oyo and Agoueh Tha R Oyo, loas of the sea, welcome
bathers on Mondays and Fridays.

Children who sleep poorly, have worms, or a poor appetite, are
bathed by the houn'gan. The houn'gan plunges the child into a basin
of water in which he has previously mashed leaves of the *mimosa
pudica* plant, called *honte* in Créole, which means "shame." This

plant has the virtue of halting attacks of fever or other pathological conditions: the malady disappears because it feels "shame'! Often the water is mixed with clairin, all or part of which was previously set ablaze—a process believed to destroy all disease germs. When the bath is finished, but before the water is poured into a hole or thrown into the sea, the vessel which contained the water is "paid;" that is to say, a coin is placed in it to remunerate the water-spirit to whom the prayer had been addressed to protect the person given the bath.

The "charm" bath is given by the mystère Danbhalah Wédo rather than by the houn'gan, because Danbhalah is the mystère believed to have plunged into the "abyssal waters" in order to induce the "abysses" to "give birth to the world." Danbhalah is therefore the bath-giver par excellence. The bath administered by Danbhalah is always a salutary one: it attracts everything pleasant, procures all kinds of favors, reconciles the staunchest enemies, obtains jobs and promotions, and cures all sorts of incurable ailments, at any rate ailments believed to be incurable. In order that the bath may be even more advantageous, it should be taken on a Thursday, Danbhalah's day, upon the "points" of Jupiter—The mystère Québiésou Dan-Leh, who is the ravisher or charmer par excellence.

The composition of the "charm" bath requires the most agreeable elements: flowers, jasmine leaves, orgeat, pulverized sweet-almond, much perfume and *agua divina*, and champagne. The "charm" bath should be taken on three consecutive days in order to obtain its full effect.

The "Lady" bath is the bath taken under the magic auspices of Erzulie. Generally speaking, it is desirable to summon the mystère Erzulie to come in person and administer the bath, just as in the case of the "charm" bath, it is preferable to call down Danbhalah Wédo into a hounsih's head, so that the mystère himself will bathe the person for whom the bath is intended. The bath of Erzulie used to be much in vogue, but it is no longer as popular as it once was. Nowadays initiates are content to take a substitute Erzulie bath by rubbing themselves with water in which Erzulie, while possessing somebody, has herself bathed. The bath water used in this fashion is thought to produce good fortune and to cure illness. The "Lady" bath contains three bunches of basilica leaves, seven sweet peppers, a measure of *zodouvant* (Eugenia crenulata Wild) powder, *baume du commandeur,* tincture of benzoin, and Florida Water. Perfume may be added in any desired quantity, perfume being the most important element in Maîtresse Erzulie's toilette. Taken preferably once a year, this bath must be preceded and followed by the offering of a dessert to the mystère who comes to administer the bath. It is believed to be of great help in winning money; and it "walks" on the "points" of Venus.

Another bath reputed to bring good luck is the Ibo bath. One or more Ibo loas are summoned to administer the bath to those who desire it. The ingredients of the bath solution must never be changed throughout the entire magical operation, that is to say, over a period of seven days. Since the bath solution diminishes in quantity with each use, there ordinarily remains only enough to rub oneself with the last few times. The formula for this bath is as follows: a litre of blazing alcohol: a banana, sea water collected "at the islands;" mushrooms; crushed pineapple; seven holly leaves; a bottle of holy water taken from a holy water basin in a church; and perfume. The "good luck" bath "walks" on the "points" of the Sun.

In order to administer the bath to combat misfortune, the houn'gan completely disrobes the client and makes him lie on the ground. Sometimes, as a special favor, he gives him a small straw mat. The houn'gan then passes a crucifix (Legba being the Voodoo Jesus) and the tail of a codfish over his joints, beginning at the head. The nape of the neck and the jaws respectively are the places of the body where the spirits of the voudouns enter or express themselves. The houn'gan therefore commands the evil spirits to withdraw from the body of the person whom he is preparing to bathe in the name of God the Father, God the Son, and God the Holy Ghost. The houn'gan then plunges his client into water containing salt (unless sea water is available), clairin, seven vine leaves, three or seven bunches of parsley, several shallots, perfume, and several pieces of money. This bath should be a very short one, lasting no longer than two or three minutes. Moreover, it should be taken on nine successive Fridays.

In order to increase the magic power of the various baths, it is advantageous to trace on the inside or the outside of the bathtub the vèvès associated with the astral influence of the loa under whose influence the bath is administered. For example, if Erzulie descends from the astral to "mount" a "horse" for the purpose of bathing an individual, a heart, or anything that has reference to the heart, is

traced both on the inner and outer walls of the tub. In the case of
Ogou, a wrought iron grill or a sword is sketched, in accordance with
the geometric tradition inherited from Africa.

Bringing Vengeance on Enemies

Manman Brigitte, or *Mademoiselle Brigitte*, is one of the best known
and most popular loas of Haitian Voodoo. Some claim that she is the
wife of Baron Samedi, lord of the cemetery, others that she is "the
most ancient of the dead," that is to say, of the Guédés. Her tree-
reposoir is the weeping willow, the elm, or the médecinier-beni.

Although Manman Brigitte does not have her own cult, which would
require a special altar in the oum'phor, she nevertheless has an enormous number of devotees. At one time they used to go to invoke and
consult her under a particular tree that grew not far from the cross
of Baron Samedi in the principal cemetery of Port-au-Prince. At
present the government police prohibit this practice. Nevertheless,
Manman Brigitte still inhabits the cemetery, abiding not only in other
trees but in various rock piles as well. She is also called Grande
Brigitte. Her powers are immense, and her vèvès are among the most
interesting in all Voodoo.

In the principal cemetery in Port-au-Prince, where formerly people
could be seen invoking her before her favorite tree had been cut down
through the combined efforts of the police and the clergy, her clients
used to sprinkle the roots of the elm with raw clairin and wheaten
flour. They also used to present her with cornmeal and peanuts, which
they placed on the ground at the foot of the tree, promising her other
gifts if she heeded the prayers addressed to her. To invoke her the
devotees would light one or more candles and stick them on the roots
or on the lower trunk of the elm tree. The multitudes of these lighted
candles which could always be seen by this tree presented a most
unusual sight, especially at dusk. Incidentally, this practice was
originally employed in addressing prayers to the cross of Baron
Samedi, and these crosses today present much the same appearance
as the steps of old churches that are literally paved with lighted
candles. The Voodooist speaks directly to the elm tree when he addressed Grande Brigitte, just as if someone were standing before him
capable of replying. Guédé Nibho, one of the most important of the

African "dead," together with the thirty other Guédés who are his brothers, sometimes claims to be the child of Brigitte. Hence the list contains thirty-one Guédés. However, more than thirty-one are observed, since each Guédé may appear under many aliases; for example, Guédé Nibho is also known as Ti Puce.

Manman Brigitte's clientele is mostly made up of people who are constantly embroiled in disputes with their friends or neighbors—people who always have enemies and who are continually involved in some argument.

On the way to the cemetery to consult the mystère (said to be "the oldest of the dead," hence the wisest), the client cuts a stalk of bayahonde before presenting himself at the elm tree. As he cuts the stalk he says: "In the name of Mademoiselle Brigitte." Arriving at the tree, he pronounces the following words with an air of great authority: "Mademoiselle Brigitte, behold the lash which 'so-and-so' or 'so-and-so' has cut to strike you with." (Implication: ". . . to strike your servant who is one with yourself, since your servant is your child.") "I bring it to you that you may teach him the lesson he deserves."

If one wishes to cause misunderstanding between two people, the prayer must contain the words: ". . . that you may prevent 'A' from becoming reconciled with 'B' or 'C.' "

As the client pronounces these words—words which are immediately echoed in all the cemeteries of the world—he bends down and embraces the ground, then scoops up a bit of earth at the foot of the elm tree, usually seven handfuls. Taking some of it in the palm of his hand, he proceeds to the home of his enemy, and when he arrives he throws the cemetery dirt towards the entrance of the house, taking care not to be observed, and uttering these words: "Mademoiselle Brigitte, here is where the person lives whom I prayed to you to torment."

On the way from the cemetery to the door of his enemy's house, he must not return anyone's greeting. He may do so, however, after he has spoken the above words, and in fact, may speak to anyone he encounters, for the ritual of the magic operation has been completed. Should he return the greeting offered him en route to his enemy's house, or speak to anyone, the magic would be ineffective.

When the anticipated results of the operation have materialized, the promises made to Brigitte in the cemetery must be fulfilled immediately under pain of having the effects of the magic backfire.

The magical operation here described illustrates the magic reciprocity established between the Voodoo mystère and the devotee. It is essentially this reciprocity that confers magic power, and which deserves special prominence, since it underlies the entire mystical system of the cult.

Use of Magic Lamps

The best and simplest way to prepare an "eternal" lamp is to pour a little castor oil and olive oil in a receptacle and hang it from the ceiling in the center of the oum'phor or one's private shrine (in case the person does not have an oum'phor but serves the mystères anyway). The location in the center of the ceiling corresponds to the location of the center-post in the oum'phor which the "eternal" lamp is considered as replacing. The lamp, or its substitute, may also be placed upon the *pé* of the mystère being served.

There is no objection to adding perfume to the castor oil and olive oil, but before adding anything else, it is advisable to wait until the mystère has made known his wishes in the matter, unless, of course, the person who prepares the lamp has professional knowledge of the necessary ingredients relative to the mystère in question. However, despite the superior knowledge of the houn'gan who prepares a lamp of this sort, the loas may appear and demand the addition of a particular powder or favorite leaf that will precipitate the virtues of the light through their contribution to the power of the elements which produce it. For example, if *baume du commandeur* is added to the oils which produce the light, the lamp will shed a lovely atmosphere of peace over the house where the lamp hangs or is placed. If, on the other hand, gunpowder or pepper is added, the domestic scene will be disturbed.

The "Work" Lamp

A "work" lamp is employed for more personal reasons. Its purpose is to obtain employment for its maker. It is placed under the aegis of Legba, since the tradition reveals that Legba is the mystère who obtains work for Danbhalah. However, the same lamp may be placed under the auspices of one or more subordinate mystères, summoned to do a piece of work and possessing the houn'gan himself or somebody else.

When properly composed, this lamp has remarkable properties. But it must be remembered that its ingredients draw their magic properties in the first place only from the analogies they bear to the results which the lamp is supposed to produce. For example, if the houn'gan wishes to cure sick people he should add some basic medicines to the lamp oil.

The lamp then summons or attracts patients. To retain his clientele, magic analogy requires that he include in the lamp a few drops of strong glue or bits of gum arabic. The lamp also grants the houn'gan the powers of the loas under whose protection it is placed. If he wants the lamp to attract patients immediately, he must add seven measures of "red precipitate" (red oxide of mercury).

Most of the "work" lamps are of a type that might be called universal, that is to say, they contain universal properties. Into their composition go numerous, somewhat diverse ingredients: olive oil, castor oil, precipitate, *baume du commandeur*, various essential oils, preferably essence of rose, a piece of beef heart, and seven packets of needles or seven needles placed upon a piece of parchment lining the bottom of the lamp. The beef heart is often punctured before being removed from the animal. The lamp also contains wine spirits, juice of the *ave* leaf, red wine, gunpowder, powdered madder, and pure lard; furthermore, these seven articles should be purchased in seven different shops in seven different parts of town.

Apart from the protection accorded this type of lamp by Legba Ati-Bon, it is frequently placed under the aegis of Loko Ati-sou Poun'goueh, of Papa Ogou, or of Papa Danbhalah. Traditionally, the lamp is placed upon the *pé* of the mystère under whose protection it lies. In times past, the lamp used to be hung in the tree-reposoir of the mystère—a custom which no longer seems to prevail, owing, no doubt, to the practical difficulties involved. The manner of rendering it most efficacious now consists in placing it at the base of some object into which it is possible to summon the desired mystère.

The best magic results are obtained from a lamp if prayers are said in front of it always at the same moment of the day or night, while the oil is being replenished, should this be necessary. The stroke of noon is the best time if the lamp is intended to achieve a beneficial aim; midnight, if its purpose is evil. While the person is reciting his prayer, he mentions his desires, at the same time stirring the contents of the lamp with a green twig. The lamp is ordinarily kept lighted until the request has been fulfilled—six, eight, ten months, or even a year, if necessary. The proper use of the lamp requires that it not be extinguished until satisfaction is obtained. If it is directed against an enemy, means should be found of secreting it at the gate of the enemy's yard.

The Black Lamp

The "black" lamp is composed of castor oil, *piment-chien*, Guinea-pepper, powdered lizard, powder of a decomposed corpse, precipitate, and soot. Preferably it is hung in the yard instead of being left in the house. This magic lamp serves mainly to compel a recalcitrant tenant to evacuate the house that he rents, an enemy to move out of the neighborhood or out of town, to produce discord in politics and public affairs, to disrupt a family, or to cause an enemy to lose his job or even to die.

If the lamp is intended to mitigate an evil, it should be placed under the auspices of a loa of the Rada rite, but if it is to serve evil ends, it comes under the jurisdiction of a Pethro loa. The lamp is made either of half a dried coconut shell, half a pumpkin, or the shell of a sea-crab. Its ingredients should be renewed every Friday for seven consecutive weeks.

The "black" lamp is most often placed under the protection of Agoueh R Oyo, the god of the sea, for when it has produced satisfactory results, either its contents are thrown into the sea or the entire lamp is placed on a tiny raft and floated out to sea where it sinks like a toy boat.

The "Bottle" Lamp or "Black Bottle"

This lamp is composed in much the same way as the last one, that is to say, according to the laws of analogy. It corresponds with the powers of a Voodoo mystère chosen because of his analogical similarities to the lamp's contents. For example, Ogou is chosen because he is associated with fire, Agoueh with water, Erzulie with love and justice. The lamp, or strictly speaking a bottle inside of which a wick is lighted but snuffed out when the bottle is corked, is hung at one end of the yard. Every day at the same hour the houn'gan, armed with a whip, rushes at the bottle and administers a sound thrashing to it. This has the effect of hastening the mystère in the performance of his assigned task.

The "Charm" Lamp

The "charm" lamp is generally placed upon a table at which the person performs the magical operations. It is usually made of half a coconut shell, and contains ingredients which have analogous qualities of sweetness and attraction: a magnet, syrup, sugar, honey, perfume and flower petals, particularly those of jasmine and heliotrope.

The chief constituent of the lamp is a sheep's brain purchased with the idea in mind of purchasing the individual whom one wishes to charm. Olive oil is added, and the lamp is lighted in the name of Legba, who represents the heart, and Erzulie, who represents the sentiment of love. It is kept lighted until results are obtained.

The "Disaster" Lamp

The "disaster" lamp is employed for Machiavellian purposes. Its two principal ingredients are lime juice and the gall bladder of an ox. To this is added raw, unrefined castor oil and soot.

This lamp is usually placed in a hole in the ground. Its constituents are placed in a dirty cooking pot, or if they are already held in another container, the whole lamp is placed in an old pot, and this is placed at the bottom of a hole dug at the foot of a tree consecrated to some mystère in a remote spot in the garden. Inasmuch as this lamp is under the aegis of the Guédé loas, gods of the cemetery, it is capable of producing dire catastrophes.

Using Blood Sacrifices

The Voodoo initiate increases his power to bring forth the gods or call back the dead by tasting the offerings that are made—even the blood of the animal sacrifices—and by swallowing a part of the material with which he traces the diagrams. This he does at the moment of placing the sacrifice upon the sign of the cross in the diagram. However, if the cross has been traced upon the ground, he buries the sacrifice in this spot. He then consumes a small portion of the food, thereby sharing it with the invisibles; whereupon (or at some time previous) he digs a hole and buries it, repeating his request at the same time.

However, before burying the sacrifices, the celebrant must make three turns with them around the hole in each direction, saying:

(1) "In the name of Bha"

(2) "In the name of Dan"

(3) "In the name of Lah"

He consequently makes six turns in all about the hole, three in one direction, three in the other. The turns to the left signify that he arises to the Orient—the East—of the magical operation, to obtain the power and the grace which he needs. The turns to the right signify that he returns from the Orient to the Occident—the West—in possession of this power and grace. The sacrifice should be dispatched into the Invisible accompanied by a few pieces of money, and it must be consecrated in the following traditional manner:

(1) orient, then sprinkle it, making the sign of the cross;

(2) make the sign of the cross over it with flour;

(3) place over it three piles of "food" in the form of a triangle;

(4) sprinkle it with the ritual beverages;

(5) cause part of it to be eaten upon the "key points" of the vèvè.

When offerings other than water are used, the celebrant orients them, strikes them three times against the ground which is to receive them, and says:

"Ké Ecumalé Gba, ku dyo."

Then, after he has declared his wishes, he buries the offerings on the spot where, at the beginning of the operation, he had made the sign of the cross upon the ground.

The volatile essence released by the act of sacrificing corresponds to the dove of the holy spirit descending "upon" or "in the head" of the celebrant at the moment he "casts the water." The descent of the holy spirit is identified supernaturally with the magic conferment of powers and favors sought by the person who controls the omnipotence. The offerings which are made to the earth, in addition to the water, conform to the special tastes of certain members of the pantheon of the invisibles. Thus, in order to bring about the appearance of a spirit more easily, one must attract it magically by offering what it wants, for example, clothes to wear when it makes its appearance, food, songs, a weapon, beverages, and perfumes—factors which constitute the "chain of magnetic attraction."

Contrariwise, to remove a loa from a given place, the houn'gan does the exact opposite of what he did to attract it. He produces the most disagreeable sounds possible. He spreads foul odors. He insults it, even striking it. He dismisses it with harsh words and chills it by pouring water over it in the name of the holy spirit.

In cases in which the celebrant does not desire to invoke all the loas of the pantheon, but to restrict his invocation to a single loa, he employs only the diagram of this one loa.

In the especially important instance in which the celebrant offers blood as a sacrifice to an invisible, it is preferable that he include, in addition to the magic diagram of the mystère invoked, that of the mystère who controls the blood, for the latter is the complementary opposite of Legba Ati-Bon (Legba Adingban), the invisible who is invoked first to "open the gates" of the fluid of the earth.

The mystère who controls the circulation of the blood is identified with the female genital organs, because the menstrual periods of the woman are affected by the blood and "walk" cabalistically upon silver; while Legba, on the other hand, is identified with the male genital organs which "walk" cabalistically upon gold. Hence the golden pin symbolizes the magician in his omnipotence, and the chain the magic itself of the operation. Therefore, the silver chain is the magic chain of the astral light.

Legba gives; Erzulie receives. So when Legba "raises" or accomplishes the sacrifice to fulfill the wish of the celebrant, the mystère who controls the blood is useful to him, if not indispensable, because this mystère allows the sacrifice to be accomplished by directing the blood of the victim into the hidden places of the terrestrial fluid under the sign of purity, which is his own attribute. The mystère who controls the blood can do anything. She is known as Erzulih (Aze-ï-Lih), and her assistance is solicited by calling her three time or six times over her diagram, which is one of her numerous astral ectoplasms. This mystère, the controller of the sacrificial blood, is the tenth sign of the oracular alphabet of the loas, and it corresponds to the rising of the sun. To invoke this power and to render it beneficent, one must say:

"By the power of Madame la Lune (Mrs. Moon), La Belle Vénus (The Fair Venus), in the name of the woman Brillant-Soleil (Brilliant Sun), in the name of SAH-MEJI, Madame Magie (Mrs. Magic) who precedes Loso-Méji (the mystère who takes the vèvè and the wish of the celebrant and transports them to the sky), in the name of Nègresse Gba-à-Dou, Nègresse Loko, Nègresse Yalodé, Nègresse Lihsah, Nègresse l'Arc-en-ciel (Rainbow), Maîtresse Agoueh-Tha-Oyo, Maîtresse La Sirène, Maîtresse La Baleine;

"By the power of Maîtresse Erzulih Fraeyja Danhomé, Nègresse Imamou Ladé, Nègresse Fréda Rada Congo Pethro Nago Caplaou Ibho, Nègresse Fréda-sih Fréda, Lih Fréda-sih Fréda and l'Fréda Lih Danhomé in agreement, Lih Can, Nègresse Fla voudoun' Cisafleur voudoun' Nègresse Thabor Mangnan Voudé, Nègresse Cibracan, Nègresse Cordon Bleu (Blue Ribbon), Nègresse Coquille Dorée (Gilded Cockleshell), Nègresse l'Océan."

In the Pethro-Zazi rite there are three ways of killing a cock offered as a sacrifice:

I.   (1) Orientation (presentation to the four cardinal points);
      (2) Rubbing the victim against all sides of the center-post;
      (3) Sprinkling with alcohol (or kerosene);
      (4) Making the sign of the cross with flour;
      (5) Plucking the crop, and sticking some of the down upon the socle, the post, and the ceremonial utensils with blood taken from the bird's throat after tearing out the tongue;
      (6) Signing with the cross the plucked neck with flour, sprinkling it with liquid, and holding it momentarily over the "strong points" of the vèvè;
      (7) Cutting the throat with a knife, but not enough so as to prevent the bird from breathing and tasting grain which is offered it; then severing the head and pouring the blood on

and around the post (as well as on the iron tongs which are found planted before the post or, more commonly, in the yard in the center of a brazier), to which the delicate crop feathers are stuck with the bird's own blood, and finally pouring the blood upon the ground over the flour-traced vèvè;

(8) Placing the bird on the ground, whence it will be taken to be cooked. Upon removal, the sacrificed cock is struck three times on the ground.

II. (1) The cock is given something to eat on the ground while the drums beat; (it is not tied up);

(2) Sprinkling of victim and vèvè with liqueurs and other alcoholic beverages reserved for the ceremony;

(3) Making the sign of the cross over the bird with flour;

(4) Orientation;

(5) Breaking the feet and the wings (one for each of the cardinal points);

(6) Plucking the crop and placing the down upon the socle;

(7) Rubbing the victim against all sides of the center-post;

(8) The second sprinkling with alcohol;

(9) Making the sign of the cross over the bird with the liqueurs and the food offerings which accompany the sacrifice;

(10) Holding the bird over the "strong points" of the vèvè;

(11) Twisting the neck as though winding a spring: the houn'gan holds the bird by the head and swings it with a circular motion until the head is torn off (or nearly so) by the tortion.

III. Illustrating the slaying of the victim by the mystère Ogou Balin'dio:

(1) The mystère moves back and forth with the bird before the centerpost (on the side facing east);

(2) He breaks the neck;

(3) he orients, then breaks the feet and wings;

(4) he tears off the head with his teeth, having first rubbed the bird upon the vèvè which had been traced with flour on the ground of the oum'phor;

(5) he throws it upon the vèvè on the ground and sprinkles the vèvè with liqueurs.

Human Sacrifice

Voodoo initiates call those who have abandoned the tradition *cabrit thomazos* (also known as "Congos and Ibos enchained"). They are members of the so-called "red" or "criminal" sects who shed human blood for sacrificial offerings.

The "red sects" are a type of survival of the secret sects of Africa whose members believe themselves to be animals—mysterious representations of the totems of clans. The members of these sects are "mounted" or "possessed" by these totem protectors in whose skins they perform extraordinary feats. They may become leopardmen, serpentmen, elephantmen, owlmen, pythonmen, crocodilemen, wolfmen, or lionmen.

The werewolves of Haiti are men or women transformed magically into birds of prey that fly in the air like real birds. During their nocturnal flight their bodies give off a luminous trail as well as an odor of hot iron or, some say, of sulfur. They pounce upon those whom they wish to capture, and carry them off into the air as a vulture carries off a hare.

The "red sects," who lean toward the Pethro rite of Voodoo, bear such diverse names as *Cochons sans poils* (Hairless Pigs), *Bissages* or *Bi-sango*, *Cochons Gris* (Gray Pigs), and *Vin'Bain-Ding* (Blood, Pain, Excrement). Their emblem is the destroying sword of St. Michael, which corresponds in astrology to the sword of Orion in the Zodiac, or the bow of Sagittarius. Grouped into sects devoted to ritual destruction, they make use of the sword and the bow in accomplishing their purposes. Tradition holds that they once dressed in white. Today, however, they prefer to wear blood-red. They also wear a curious silver ring ornamented with a tower.

Members of these sects have become ritual destroyers through a false concept of crucifixion. They believe that Legba, the Voodoo Jesus, died upon the *arbre sec* (the center-post or the cross) in order to serve as an edible human sacrifice, a concept which they are encouraged to hold because of the expression employed in the very churches that oppose them: "This is my Body . . . This is my Blood." The Voodoo tradition accuses the "red sect" of having put Jesus to death as a human sacrifice.

The expression *cabrit thomazo* refers to the "impure" Voodooists because of the serpent of the Afro-Judaic temple that is known as *Asch*, *Ast*, or *Ast-Hom*. *Ast-Hom* is believed by traditionalists to be a variation of *Thom-As*, a later African expression signifying "the musical atmosphere of the oum'phor."

Members of the various "red" sects are under the fearful influence of Erzulie Zan-dor, who substitutes for the serpent a man who, according to the sect and the locality, is called Legba Ati-Bon, Is, or Ahou-râ Mazda.

Some ill-informed writers attribute the origin of the "red" sects to the cannibalistic character of the Mandingue, Mondongue, and Bissango tribes from whom the Bandor mystères were inherited. Tradition, however, holds that the schism dates from the historic disagreement between the Samaritans and the Jews.

7

Rituals and Ceremonies of Voodoo

MANY of the colorful and exciting rituals and ceremonies of Voodoo are basically designed to help lead the houn'sihs to the light. In a moment we will go into some oum'phors to observe a few of these ceremonies in detail. But first it would be helpful to scan in outline form some of the basic rituals:

Metté n'anme (Placing the soul)—a process which magically balances the *ba* and the *ka* of the newborn, that is, the two parts of the soul.

Lévé nom (Taking the name)—talisman and magic protection given to children. They consist in taking the name of an ancestor in order to perpetuate the tradition. The child is entrusted to the protective spirit whose name he has taken.

Garde (Protection)—magic confirmation of the *Lévé nom*—the loa to which a person is entrusted and to which the person must devote ritual sacrifices as a compensation for the protection. The protected one thus "serves" the loa. This ceremony may take place at any age.

Lavé-tête (Washing the head)—ritual baptism, to facilitate by means of water or any other liquid, the entrance of the loas "in the head" of the new initiate, water being the pathway of the loas.

Can-Zo, or *Boulez-Zain:* initiatory "putting to bed" on the "houn'sih-point," or "ordinary putting to bed"—(a) Initiatory "putting to bed" in the *djévò* (lavé-tête); (b) Food offered to the head (manger-tête); (c) Can-zo, properly so-called (Initiation by fire); (d) Coming forth of the initiated houn'sih (lever); (e) Baptism; (f) Putting on of the ritual necklace.

Rafraîchi-tête (Refreshing the head)—a further baptism for reinforcing the maître-tête loas by opening wider for them the pathway of the spirit by the magical power of water.

Haussements (Lifting, or rising)—ceremonies of the granting of initiatic degrees, including the successive degrees to which the houn'sih can-zo, La Place, Houn'guénicon, Confiance, Mambo, Houn-'gan, and others may attain.

Dé-sou-nin—recovery of the powers of deceased initiates.

Prise du mort—obtaining the spirit of the dead from the cemetery where the person has been buried.

Boulez-zain mort Ou-an Zain—a ceremony performed once or three times, according to the degree held by the deceased.

Ouetté mort l'an d'l'eau Cassez-canari—magic ceremonies in which the souls of deceased Voodooists are withdrawn from the depths of the water in order that they may evolve metempsychically.

All these ceremonies have reference fundamentally to three vital plans:

(1) *OLO-KOU-IN'-WÉ:* This concerns the Voodooist from the age of 1 to 10 years. This plan is connected with the seminal water (the water that mounts), symbolized by the ritual bath of Danbhalah Wédo. The child who belongs to the tradition must be placed under the protection of Legba by means of amulets, scapulars, and philacteries: Legba A-Gbo-Gbo or Legba Abôbô, who protects him from all evil-doing.

(2) *OLO-SIH-SÉ:* This concerns the Voodooist from the age of 10 to 21 years. It is concerned with the "mounting of the ritual water" in the form of Dan Wédo, the serpent painted on the post of Legba. The Voodooist is therefore removed from his position on the first plan where he had profited from the starting ceremonies like the *Metté n'anme* and the first *Lavé Tête*, now to be placed under the protection of Legba Sé-Gbo-Lih-Sah, who is superior to Legba A-Gbo-Gbo. This displacement takes place as a *haussement* (a raising, or lifting), because the water begins to "rise" in the form of the serpent, beginning

with the socle of the post (*sah*) and going towards the astral light of
the star of Ifé (*Lih*). The houn'*sih* is therefore thought to go to Ifé
in search of his soul (*sé*) through the channel of the post (*lih-sah*).
The plan includes the central ceremonies like the *can-zo*, for these
ceremonies involve the knowledge that flows down from the star, and
which later the houn'gan will be seen to confer when he goes to Ifé
under the conduct of his initiators to take the asson.

(3) *OLO-RUN TI-TÉ:* This concerns the houn'sih from the age of
21 years until death. It is concerned with Voodoo omniscience relative
to the powers of the "water which rises." These powers take the name
of Maîtresse Erzulie, and enable the initiate to learn the science that
causes the water to rise and descend in the form of the serpent of
Voodoo—that is to say, to summon the loas ritually and to utilize them
as physicians, counsellors, protectors, runners, generals, initiators,
magi, sorcerers, and transmutators. The Voodoo initiate is accordingly
considered as being "in the wood" of the center-post, and therefore
finds himself under the influence of *Legba-i-Toto*—an affectionate
name given to the ritual post. When Voodoo initiates die, they find
themselves already in Ifé. This assimilation teaches why all ancestors—
houn'sih, houn'guénicon, la place, mam'bo, houn'gan—return to Ifé at
their death as powers and as Voodoo loas, since it is in Ifé where they
have been to take the asson, or the initiatory grades that precede the
taking of the asson. This third plan—the master plan—includes essentially the "taking of the asson." It is the plan of the complete initiation
from the grades of la place and hou'guénicon to the grades of mam'bo
and of houn'gan.

Invigorating The Gods

On this night great events are about to take place—sacred rites that
are performed only once every two years. The most important ghost-
gods of Voodoo will be called out of the Haitian darkness to mount
the bodies of the chosen, and they will be reinvigorated with sacrifices
and mysterious rituals to strengthen their powers of granting the
prayers of their followers.

The gathering place is the oum'phor, presided over by Ramise. She
has been a mam'bo—an empress of Voodoo—for many years. Her great

powers are known far and wide. Among her guests tonight are many who have traveled great distances to attend.

As night closes in many people mill about in the courtyard, continually coming and going. The horses of distant visitors are tied up near the entrance gate. Vendors of fried food, candy, and wine-and-herb drinks called *trempés* offer their wares spread out on portable trays. Large trees—the resting places of the ghost-gods—form shadowy masses at the edges of the courtyard. At the foot of the trees candles glow here and there. The low buildings of the oum'phor compound extend into the darkness to the thatched dwellings of Ramise's family and those of other members of her Voodoo Society.

The peristyle of the oum'phor is illuminated by several small kerosene lamps fastened together and hung like chandeliers on either side of the center-post that holds up the gallery's thatched roof. The post has been freshly painted with vivid colors, matching decorations on the walls. These decorations surround a large inscription that reads *Société La Fleur cé nous*—We Are the Flower Society. Below this appears the cult name of Ramise—*Soutini Ladé, Mam'bo Da-Guinin*.

Many houn'gans and mam'bos arrive with their houn'guénicons and houn'sihs, as is the custom. All take their places inside the peristyle on chairs or benches reserved for them.

The ceremony commences about eight o'clock in the evening with the usual opening chants. Three drums of the Rada rite are placed along one side, and behind them the houn'sihs are seated on benches. Legba is greeted with the seven traditional chants sung in his honor by which he is implored to open the barrier of the spirits and to permit the living to communicate with the mystères. The rest of the loas are then greeted in hierarchic order.

Presently Ramise comes out of the bagui holding a jug of water. She advances to the center of the peristyle, orients the jug, and approaches the drums. She salutes them, as well as the *ogan* (a musical instrument that is a kind of bell), by sprinkling water three times in front of each. After the *bô tè* (genuflecting and kissing the ground), she turns to the center-post and salutes it by sprinkling water three times as before and kissing it three times.

All the houn'sihs, robed in white and standing in close formation, salute the four cardinal points together with Ramise. They turn around in place, bending their knees in quiet reverence in accordance with the sacred Voodoo greeting.

Pethro, Congo, and Rada drums.

Ritual flag.

Temporary altar in an oum'phor's yard.

Voodoo-sih possessed by a loa.

Dishes for the Maraça spirits.

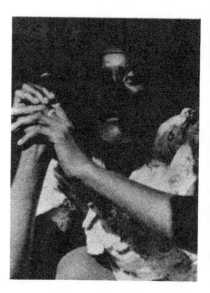

Voodoo priestess (mam'bo).

The Assato drum.

Voodoo drums.

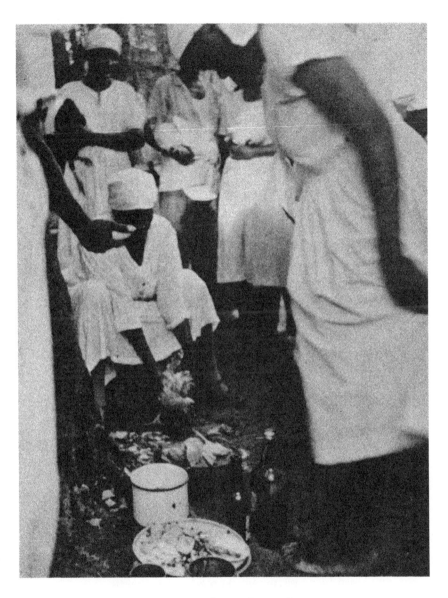

Women tending to the ritual pots.

The black bottle on the Central Post contains liquid
used by priests to multiply powers of the spirits.

Ceremonial tray.

Houn'sih blowing the *lambi* to call the wind which will take the ship to Aux Ilets (a magic location out at sea).

The ceremonial tray on beach, surrounded by voodoo diagrams and pictures.

The ship of Agoueh en route to Aux Ilets, accompanied by the conical drums and a ritual flag.

The sacred white sheep headed for the ship.

The ceremonial steersman.

Ritual hens and pigeons, before being sacrified into the sea.

The tray of ritual offerings,
in the main of the ship.

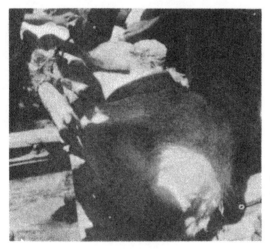

The sheep, just before
being sacrificed.

The houn'sih placing the tray in the sea.

The sheep as it is being thrown to the sea.   The tray capsizing with the sacred dishes.

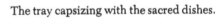

Voodoo drums before the departure for Ife.
(In the background, the author taking notes.)

Ritual bed made of banana-tree leaves representing Ife, where drums are symbolically sent to renew their magic powers.

The priest "feeds" the sacred drums to strengthen them.

Then Ramise, turning to the houn'gan Norvilus from whom she long ago "took the asson," hands him the water jug with ritual gestures, and he in turn salutes the mambo. The jug is passed from hand to hand among all the visiting houn'gans and mam'bos. The houn'sihs come forth in pairs, lined up according to their degree of initiation, turn around and kiss the ground before the drums and the center-post. Next, while the houn'gans and mam'bos exchange ritual greetings to the accompaniment of rattling assons, the houn'sihs curtsey in pairs first before Ramise, then before each ranking member of the company. They then turn in a circle upon one another leaning their heads together. The greetings differ according to the hierarchic degree of the member of the society addressed. The mam'bo is saluted three times by each pair of houn'sihs who curtsey before her and kiss the ground. She takes them by the hand, assists them to their feet, and helps them to make three graceful turns. The peristyle becomes a whirl of white dresses—white being *de rigueur* this evening.

As soon as the chants honoring the loa Sobo are heard, the door of the inner chamber of the oum'phor is flung wide open for the sortie of the flags:

Papa Sobo lan houmfor;	Papa Sobo who is in the oum'phor;
li mandé drapeaux.	he asks for the flags.
Drapeau cilà, éloué.	That flag, éloué.
Papa Sobo lan houmfor;	Papa Sobo who is in the oum'phor;
li mandé drapeau loa'm lan.	he asks for the flags of that loa.
O drapeau-çà, éloué.	Oh that flag, éloué.

Immediately the houn'sihs arrange themselves in two rows. From the wide open door come two women in long white dresses, barefoot, each bearing a splendid flag of embroidered velvet with designs worked in pailettes. *La place*, a long antique sabre in his hand, leads the way. They come out backwards, turning in circles. La place is a young man, tall, slender, and very lithe, and he advances to the almost dance-like air of the ritual march customarily performed on such occasions. The movements are smooth and easy, without jerks, beginning from the shoulders and continuing down to the knees which bend in cadence. Mindful of his duty, la place leads the two flag-bearers around the center-post; then slowly at first, but with increasing speed, his sabre pointed and the flags unfurled and waving, he proceeds to salute the drums.

He now returns to the center-post and salutes it "to the four faces."
He kisses the post three times, then leads the two flag-bearing houn-
'sihs over to the mam'bo who, asson and bell in hand, faces la place,
who points his sabre towards the ground, and the two flag-bearers
standing on either side of him. Nearly the entire length of the peristyle
separates them. They kneel before the mam'bo three times in a quick
curtsey, with a slight bending of the knees and their hips thrust backwards, to the rattling and tinkling of the asson and the bell which is
shaken at each salute. In a quadrille-like figure the group forms and
reforms four times, in such a way that the mam'bo receives the salutation at the four cardinal points. Finally, la place advances alone to
the mam'bo and, with one knee on the ground he offers her the sword
hilt to kiss, while he in turn kisses the ground. With one hand she
assists him to his feet and guides him in making the three ritual turns.
The first flag-bearer then comes forward, and with full and gracious
movements passes her blue and red silk embroidered flag over Ramise's
head. Three times she advances and retires; then advancing on her
knees three long paces, she presents the flag to be kissed at the top of
the staff, while she herself kisses the ground. She is helped to her feet
as la place was, whereupon the second flag-bearer comes forward.
   The same ceremonial takes place before each houn'gan and mam'bo
present. At length all the houn'sihs are invited to come forward, kneel,
and kiss the sabre and the flags.
   After the singing of several chants, three houn'gans come out of the
inner chamber of the oum'phor advancing backwards and holding
their assons. All three are of the same height—tall and slender—and
they move with slow steps, their assons rattling incessantly. One of
them holds a lighted candle. They give the impression of attracting
and drawing towards themselves something which cannot as yet be
clearly seen, something there in the darkness of the inner oum'phor
which requires the combined power of all three houn'gans to bring it
forth. Now the *confiance* enters the peristyle, his white clothes scarcely
visible under all the long strings of multicolored *canzo* necklaces that
he wears about his neck, some crossed over the breast, some hung from
the shoulder, others over the arm—a heavy, moving mass of cold-
sparkling colors. His eyes are closed; his dark, round face expression-
less and held high. He staggers, intoxicated by the mystères; he turns,
reels, jerks, hops backwards on one foot. The asson calls him, insistent;
the chants rise louder, breaking into a regular fanfare. Soon he moves

closer to the center-post, the heavy necklaces swinging with his movements and clinking against one another. He collides with the others,
stumbles, seeming almost to lose his balance, and performs gyrations
impossible to perform in his normal state.

The three houn'gans lead the confiance to the center of the peristyle
where he falls heavily on his knees. Ramise and Norvilus begin to re-
lieve him of his colorful load of necklaces. When the necklaces are no
longer on his shoulders, he regains consciousness and, still dizzy, kisses
the ground and gets on his feet.

La place and the flag-bearers kneel before the mam'bo who hands
each houn'sih a necklace and a *agouéssan*, a white cloth band that is
passed over one shoulder and knotted at the opposite hip. The
agouéssans and necklaces are worn crosswise front and back. Each
necklace is different from all the others, as its colors must match those
identified with its owner's personal loas.

One after the other the houn'sihs kneel and receive their ritual
adornments, kiss the ground at the mam'bo's feet, and arise. Once
again they all fall into rank near the center-post while the call-to-order
chants and the repeated shouts of "Abobo!" resound.

A confiance brings the mam'bo a white plate containing cornmeal,
on top of which reposes an egg. The cornmeal will be used in tracing
the vèvès. In the other hand he holds a lighted candle and a pot of
water with which Ramise draws a circle around the center-post and
makes a trail of water leading directly to the door of the oum'phor
holy of holies.

Having oriented the plate and the candle that she holds with both
hands, Ramise pronounces the ritual invocation, raising her arms in a
gesture of great reverence, and proceeds to the task of tracing the
vèvè, while appropriate chants are made by the chorus:

 O vèvè, Voudoun vè, Bon Dié O!
 O vélà Kounn tié. Vélà Kounn tié!
 Danbhalah Wédo Kounn tié!

A second Yanvalou song directly follows the first:

 O miton ver, Danbhalah Wédo,
 O miton ver, Ai-Da Wédo,
 Lada yé, O miton ver, Lada yé.

The design of the vèvè is very complex and includes the symbols of
many mystères drawn around seven circles, on each of which a zin, or
pot, will soon be placed. It occupies nearly all the free space around

the center-post. When the vèvè is completed, seven tiny reed chairs are set in front of the circles indicated for the zins. A chant calling the hun'sih-canzos is given by the houn'guénicon. Then the houn'sihs proceed to the djévô, or initiation chamber, where all the necessary accoutrements for the *boulé-zin ceremony*, which we are witnessing, have been prepared. On the floor of the *djévô*, spread out on a layer of leaves, is a straw mat covered with a white cloth. On the mat lie bundles of pine wood, leaves of mombin-franc and laloguinin, white china plates (one for each zin), knives, spoons, forks, and spotlessly clean glasses and napkins; likewise a measure of wheat flour, a large *coui*, or calabash dish, full of cornmeal, bottles of olive oil, liqueur, rum, couis of corn grains and roasted peanuts, ground corn, chopped raw food (called the *mangé-dior*), a coui containing the *acras-nagos* (small cornmeal balls which were prepared before the ceremony), and a plate of *acassan* (a thick beverage of cornmeal and syrup). As many chickens as there are zins lie upon the mat. Usually these are young birds. A pile of large wrought-iron spikes used to make tripods for the clay zins and the iron Nago zin completes the list. In an earlier ceremony, all the zins had been "signed with the cross." The mam'bo, asson and bell in hand, had pronounced the ritual invocations to the principal mystères of her oum'phor. She had also consecrated the zins by drawing the vèvès of these mystères on their sides in chalk, not omitting the *milocan*—a composite vèvè for all the mystères. Only the Nago vèvès are drawn on the cast-iron zin. The pottery zins are designated for the living (*zins vivants*) or for the dead (*zins morts*). This evening two zins are reserved for the dead. Around the vèvès and on the inner sides of the zins numerous small crosses are marked.

When the houn'sihs reach the djévô they kneel in pairs before a houn'gan or a confiance, who orients and gives them their loads. They kiss the ground and rise. Gradually the cortège forms, its entrance into the peristyle suggesting a ballet formation. La place, sabre in hand, opens the way by making three ritual turns on the threshhold. All the houn'sihs make similar turns. A slow wheeling of white dresses brightens the dimness of the peristyle. The flags unfurl, wave and revolve about the mam'bo who approaches majestically, asson and bell in hand. The three houn'gans follow her at a short distance holding the lighted candle and the pot of water. The drums go wild with their beating and booming, the chorus bursts into song, while the rattling assons are heard above everything else. Facing the houn'sihs, the

Confiance proceeds backwards with a chicken in each hand, "fanning" them with sweeping movements of his arms. He dances with snake-like contortions leading out the houn'sihs in single file, each of them bearing a particular article of the ritual paraphernalia. Some carry bundles of pinewood sticks apron-fashion in their white skirts. Others bear armfuls of mombin branches. Some hold pitcher-shaped, amphora-like bottles. Still others are loaded with enormous iron spikes, or carry *couis* on their heads, bracing them gracefully with uplifted arms. Large cane baskets are heaped with all the other materials that will be needed for the ceremony. Each zin is entrusted to a houn'sih canzo who carries it with great care.

Chant follows chant in the cool night, while the drums beat and resound in unison. The mam'bo, surrounded by the flags and escorted by la place, approaches the foot of the center-post. The Confiance swings the flapping chickens up and down. He takes several steps, always backwards, while the line of houn'sihs pretends to advance. Three times, in accordance with the old Guinin (African) rite, the cortège must pretend to start, each time retracing its steps, always facing the mam'bo. At length they all slowly move into the peristyle singing. They make a turn about the center-post in a special kind of undulating dance, two steps to the right, two steps to the left.

The houn'guénicon, standing at the foot of the center-post, seems inspired, sending one chant after the other. Most of the houn'sihs, more or less "mounted" by their mystères, come forth with their eyes almost closed, reeling, turning about the vèvès, yet careful not to step on them and spoil them.

The officiants who are going to "burn the zins" take their places on the small low chairs. The houn'sihs who brought in the ritual materials, one after the other, slowly kneel before the mam'bo, orient their loads, and place them on the ground. Alongside each of the places in the vèvè designated by a circle a zin is placed together with its proper ritual materials. The bundles of pinewood and mombin leaves are heaped at the base of the socle.

The prayers are about to begin. The seven houn'gans and mam'bos, each of whom will shortly be in charge of burning a zin, are seated on the small chairs holding their assons. The dancing has stopped, and all around them the houn'sihs make a circle, sitting on their heels or upon mats, kneeling or squatting, forming a mass of white dresses that press close upon the ritual designs traced on the bare ground. Bowing her head and covering her eyes with one hand, Ramise begins the prayers amid deep silence.

First come Roman Catholic prayers, then hymns intoned in a nasal voice, and finally the Voodoo prayer commences. The *Sinnd'jiô* are reeled off one after the other, interrupted only by the ritual cry "Liss adolé Zo, et Zo, et Zo!" commencing loud and growing gradually weaker, ending with

Hé ya Grand Père Eternel, sinn djiô é,
Hé ya Grand Père éternel, sinn djiô docor akoué,
Hé ya Grand Père éternel, sinn nan min bon Dieu ho sinn han.
Hé ya Marassas Guinin, sinn djiô é,
Hé ya Legba Attibon, sinn djiô é.

All the names of the Guinin (African) mystères are recited one after the other in fixed order, and always at rhythmic intervals the refrain:

Apô Lissabagui ouangan scié Lissa dolé Zo,
Lissa dolé Zo, et Zo, et Zo, et Zo . . .

to which the houn'sihs respond:

é Zo, é Zo, é Zo.

When the name of a mystère particularly honored in the oum'phor is mentioned, all the houn'sihs are obliged to kiss the ground. At length the *prière Guinin* (African prayer) proper begins. Long psalm-like chants are intoned by the mam'bo. Lead by the houn'guénicon, the houn'sihs give the responses in ringing tones that contrast with the subdued voice of Ramise. Occasionally the rattle of the asson is heard along with the chanting. The prayers continue a long time. Then comes the chant:

Moin yenvalou yenva, moin yenva, O corani yé.

The prayers finished, Ramise and all the others rise. Taking a jug of water she devoutly raises and orients it to the four cardinal points, pronouncing the ritual invocation. All the houn'sihs turn as one to the point saluted, and, keeping their places, repeat the gesture of salutation by slightly bending their knees. An extraordinarily solemn dignity lends the scene a profoundly religious significance. The houn'guénicon gives the prescribed chant:

O Miguel O, Mayofré, Miguel O éha Mayofré,
O Mayofré, Legba Atibon, O Mayofré, Loco Atisou,
O Mayofré, Grande Aizan Vélékété. O Miguelo, O Mayofré

The chant finished, the houn'sihs begin their dance again around the center-post under the leadership of the la Place and the flag-bearers. Sometimes the direction of the dance is changed: a certain number of turns are "given" to the right, a few to the left. The houn'gans and mam'bos are seated in their places, each assisted by a kneeling houn'sih canzo. All are barefoot in accordance with the Guinin ritual. Each houn'gan pours a little water, wine, syrup, a few grains of corn, peanuts, and bits of a biscuit in a glass that is placed next to a small candle. At this instant the chant rings out:

Ah é planté i poteau é! Legba planté i poteau é . . .

Each houn'gan takes one of the three spikes lying at his side, orients it, and hammers it into the ground with a rock. The three spikes are set in such a way as to form a tripod for the zin, called the *pieds-zin* or *poteaux-zins*. The houn'gan then receives them by orienting and pouring three times in the center of the tripod a bit of the mixture contained in the glass. The candle is lighted and likewise placed exactly in the center. These preparations are all made simultaneously by the seven houn'gans and mam'bos in front of the zins, which are then placed upon their supports. The officiants must set them on the spikes using only their bare feet. The pinewood sticks are taken up in bundles of seven, oriented, and ignited from the candle flame.

The houn'sihs continue the dance close behind one another, often with their hands placed upon the shoulders of the person in front, singing and swaying, and accentuating the rhythm in a kind of African-like quick-step march. The special songs for Legba follow immediately. A lighted pinewood stick is handed to each houn'sih as she passes.

The magic round continues. The flaming sticks form a luminous crown above the dancers who circle faster and faster. The smell of the pine pitch exuding from the burning sticks mingles with that of the ritual herbs. Intermittent flashes of light from these dozens of improvised torches give the perisyle a bizarre illumination. Eyes, teeth, and necklaces flash in the darkness.

The houn'sihs now return the pinewood sticks to the officiants who orient and slip them under the zins. A little water is poured into each, then some olive oil, syrup, and wine, and if the zins are *zins vivants* (zins for the living), a few grains of salt are added. The houn'guénicon begins a new chant:

Hé a Koklo a déni yé, Papa Legba yan ouézo o an ouézo . . .

Each houn'gan takes the young chicken at his side, orients and

crosses it, gives it a few grains of corn to peck at, and then kills it.
Some of the mam'bos break the wings and feet of the bird and force
open the beak to obtain a little blood with which to stick the feathers
plucked from the crop on the "four faces" of the zin. However, many
houn'gans claim that this act is not essential to the ritual. The birds
are killed, in accordance with the African rite, by twisting the neck
(*cou viré*), that is to say, the neck is wrung and the head torn off by
a quick twist of the hand. The bodies of the chickens are then handed
to the assisting houn'sih canzo. In a moment they are drawn, plucked,
cleaned, singed, cut in half, washed with sour oranges, and handed
back to the houn'gans and mam'bos. They are then passed over the
zins, cut into several pieces, and put in the zins to cook. Meanwhile,
the feathers are tied in little bunches that resemble small bouquets of
flowers or shaving brushes, and then are placed to one side. These will
later be used for greasing the zins.

The houn'sihs continue all the while to dance around the vèvès.
Around and around they go. Some, drunk with the loas, are staggering
and tottering, but swept along by the movement of the dance they
continue without losing their places. It is exceptional, however, to see
anyone completely possessed during this part of the ceremony. The
drums beat madly with intermittent clinking of the ogan heard in the
background.

When the chicken has been cooked, each of the houn'gans mixes oil
and red wine in a white plate. He then calls several houn'sih canzos
to his side, one at a time. He makes them dip their hands into the mixture and take a piece of chicken from the bottom of the zin. Three
times the piece is placed upon the mombin leaves before being left
there. When the last piece has been withdrawn, some ground cornmeal is placed in the zin, stirred well, and cooked in the same water
as the chicken.

In the case of the Nago zin, the first part of the ceremony is exactly
the same as for the other zins except that no chicken is required. Instead, little balls of cornmeal, called *acras Nago*, are prepared in
advance. They are cooked in the Nago zin. Then they are removed
with the same ceremony as the pieces of chicken, and placed in a *coui*
(half calabash) or on a white plate.

When the cornmeal mush in the zins has become fairly thick, the
houn'gan calls each houn'sih canzo from the dance. One by one they
kneel at his side. Each dips a hand into the mixture of oil and wine,

and then with an arm held by the houn'gan like a long wooden spoon,
scoops up a bit of the boiling hot cornmeal. She orients this, presses it
in the palm of her hand to form a ball, and places it upon the mombin
leaves. She then kisses the ground, rises, and moves aside for the next
houn'sih. This ritual is called *atoutou*. When no more cornmeal remains, the zin, hot as it is, is removed from its tripod with the soles
of the bare feet held against its sides. The Nago zin is removed in the
same manner. Although no special precautions are taken there is never
any evidence of the skin of the feet being burned.

During the entire length of this prolonged ceremony the houn'sihs
never cease to "run around the zins" (*courir les zins*), sometimes in
one direction, sometimes in the other, lead by la place and the flag
bearers. The singing continues uninterrupted, each song pertaining
to the ritual and corresponding to a particular action:

M'pr'al boulé go zin pou	I'm going to boil a big zine for
Loa Alouba.	Loa Alouba.
Ma pr'al boulé go zin,	I shall be boiling a big zin,
go zin çà, go zin Dan Ballah	this big zin, Dan Ballah Ouéddo's
Ouéddo.	big zin.

At times the zins and their attendants seem to be enclosed by a
veritable white moving wall. There are so many houn'sihs that they
move jam-packed against one another, keeping time with their feet
when movement is impeded, and bounding wildly forward as the
la place leads them on. Their bare feet strike the ground with a dull,
rhythmic, obsessive beat.

The zins are removed from their tripods, scraped clean of the last
vestige of corn with a wooden spoon, and smeared with olive oil by
means of the small feather brushes. This done, they are replaced, again
with the bare feet, on the three supporting spikes. A little more oil is
again poured in each of them and more pine wood is placed under-
neath to make a hot fire. Everyone must now wait until the zins catch
fire from the oil inside them.

The chanting redoubles its intensity. A kind of excitement increasing by the minute seizes the crowd. The houn'gans and mam'bos get
up and move aside as the heat becomes intense around the small fires.
The ground is brushed clean around each fire. The pine wood burns
brightly beneath the zins which stand out black in the midst of the
orange flames licking them on all sides. Houn'gans and mam'bos all

shake their assons over the zins while uttering the ritual words. The incantations continue. At length a zin bursts into flames. "A bobo! A bobo!" cries the enthusiastic crowd. All the houn'sihs fall on their knees and kiss the ground, singing:

Go zin moin ap' prend	My zin is catching
di feu. Ai-bobo!	fire. Ai-bobo!

One, two, three zins ignite. Other lamps are extinguished, and the flames alone light the peristyle, wildly and fantastically. The heat is suffocating, but the houn'gans and mam'bos continue their work without noticing it. "A bobo!" The dance circles faster and faster, lead by la place and the flag bearers, wheeling, turning, revolving. "A bobo!" Loas "mount" several of the women. They stumble and stagger, but keep right on dancing. A houn'gan steps out of the crowd, rattling his asson and bell, and speaking words to prevent the possessions from becoming complete. Several houn'sihs kiss the ground, get up with difficulty, and still completely dazed take their places again in the dance.

Ramise, aided by several confiances, makes her way to the inner oum'phor. She comes out carrying a "dressed up" govi in each arm. Slowly she bends down and passes them one after the other through the flames, then the other govis, *pot-de-têtes*, necklaces, and *paquets*. All the pottery zins are now on fire, and the houn'sihs remove the pine sticks from under them. They burn from their own fuel, little pots blackened and crowned with flames. Scattered on the ground, bits of hot charcoal glow red. The Nago zin has not been scraped clean like the others, and is the only one that has not caught fire. The houn'gan in charge of it comes and shakes his asson and bell over it. His somber face glows in the light of the burning coals, and a look of intense concentration is read in his set features as he utters the invocation in a low voice. Now the Nago zin bursts into flame. The houn'sihs kiss the earth, rise, and immediately give the chant in Nago rhythm. The drums beat madly.

> Tolisha Legba m'di yé,
> a hi massah i toto,
> Salué Nago yé!
> Salué Nago, Nègue Nago Royor,
> Ago Tolisha, salué Nago, yé!

Ramise quickly passes the govis and the other objects through the flames of the Nago zin, then takes a bottle of rum and pours a fair amount of it into the zin. Immediately a huge flame leaps up licking about the roof beams in a dazzling light. Ramise sprays the rum from her mouth to the four cardinal points. The possessions now commence in great numbers. Nearly all the houn'sihs are "mounted." The eyes dazzled by the blazing fires can hardly distinguish the loas moving about in all directions. Some are dancing a frenzied Nago rhythm, for the drums are never still; others roll on the ground and are helped up by one or another of the houn'gans or mam'bos. Fantastic shadows play upon the walls of the enclosure. Some of the houn'sihs in quick succession kiss the vèvès; others crowd around Ramise, now possessed by the loa Ogou Badagri. The rest are still dancing, screaming out the Nago songs lead off by the houn'guénicon who stands near the drummers:

Eh, liki liki eh;
Jean-Paul Nago; ya yé!
Liki, liki eh, Ogou Chalodé,
Liki liki o, o Nago ya;
Ogou Ashadé!

When things get a little quieter and the loas have taken their leave, the mambo gives the signal to pass the left hand and the left foot through the last flames of the zins. This ritual is known as the *Dessounin*.

When all the zins have burned out, they are removed, as before, with the bare feet. Then the spikes are pulled up, and all the ritual accessories are diligently gathered by the houn'sihs. The various foods are separated, and those that belong to the *zins vivants* (zins for the living), such as the chickens and the balls of cornmeal (the *acras Nago*), are divided among the members of the Society. The food cooked in the *zins morts* (zins for the dead) is set aside in a coui. All the ceremonial debris—mombin leaves, cold embers, charred pine-wood, feathers, and leftovers in general—are collected. The place where the *zin mort* stood is carefully cleaned, because this is where the hole is to be dug. The *zins vivants* are placed in the reposoir of Legba, that is to say, at the courtyard gate, while the Nago zin is returned to the oum'phor holy of holies.

In the cleared place a very simple vèvè is traced with ground cornmeal. It takes the form of a circle circumscribing a cross. A man comes forth carrying a *pince*—a long, pointed iron bar—which he uses to dig a hole within the area of the crossed circle, around the sides of which the dirt is piled evenly. When the hole is sufficiently deep, the sign of the cross is made over it with flour, and water is sprinkled into it together with grains of corn, peanuts, liqueur, and clairin. The food to be buried is now brought, carefully wrapped in a white napkin used in the service of the *zin mort*. The packet of food is then placed upon mombin leaves in the bottom of the hole.

The *zins morts* are broken with one of the spikes, and the pieces, together with those of the glass and the plate, are thrown into the hole. Finally, the wooden spoon and all the floor sweepings are also collected and dumped in. The houn'sihs kneel in a circle, and all together push back the dirt and fill up the hole. When this work is finished, they rise and form a circle around the hole, each houn'sih placing her hands on the shoulders of the houn'sih in front of her. With the left foot with which they begin a swaying movement forwards and backwards, they stamp the ground smooth, giving out at the same time a song with a special rhythm:

> Dia rélé Dia Dia ké ké, ké, ké dia! Dia rélé dia!
> Guédé Nibo! Dia ké ké, ké ké dia!
> Baron Samedi! Dia ké ké, ké ké dia!

These wild, hammering, obsessive sounds accompany the beating of bare feet upon the ground. In a moment the Guédés—the loas of the cemetery—begin to possess the houn'sihs. All of them are here: Guédé Nibo, Guédé Nouvavou, Guédé HounSou, Guédé Tiouaoué. Without breaking the rhythm the Guédés join in beating the ground with the others. All in the dance become "mounted." The Guédés place themselves in two lines facing each other, and, still holding each other by the shoulders, beat the soles of the left feet upon the ground to accentuate the "Dia kéké dia!" The "dias" ring out in time to reinforce the hammering of the feet.

When the ground is duly smoothed, Ramise traces a vèvè over the covered hole with ground cornmeal, and in the center of this design places a lighted candle alongside a plate called "The Adoration." Various people come forth and place small coins upon it to be used for charity the following day.

One by one the Guédés take their leave. The ceremony is nearly

ended. The necklaces of the houn'sihs are taken from the kneeling
women with the same rituals employed at their distribution, except
that the person assigned the duty of carrying them to the inner
oum'phor does so in an unobtrusive manner. Next, the flags must also
be returned to the oum'phor. The mam'bo is again given the ritual
salutation at the four cardinal points, whereupon she chants the song:

    O Goli yé, goli yé,
    oua Po-drapeau, goli yé
    O Golimin goli yé oua goli yé
    oua O Po-drapeau.
    O Po-drapeau! Po drapeau,
    ban moin lan main pour m'levé!
    O Goli yé oua, goli yé,
    oua O Po-drapeau.

This lively song accompanies la place and the two flag-bearers as
they circle the center-post, turning, whirling about, dancing, spinning
around many, many times, first to the right, then to the left. The flags
unfurl and flap in the wind as the houn'sihs bound in their dance, and
the bright sparkle of the paillettes clashes with the quick gleam of the
pointed sabre. At last la place signals that the dance is over. The doors
of the inner oum'phor are opened, and he darts ahead, sabre forward,
the flags following his lead—a mere feint. Three times he must ap-
proach the doorsill before finally turning around and entering the
oum'phor backwards. The doors are immediately closed on the procession.

It is nearly dawn, but under the peristyle the dance continues, for
all the mystères must be greeted before the lights can be extinguished.

In all the oum'phors in the region of Port-au-Prince and the Cul-de-
Sac Plain, it is customary to celebrate such a *boulé-zins caille* ceremony
as we have witnessed at more or less infrequent intervals for the purpose of "warming up" the mystères served in the oum'phor—in other
words to give them increased power to be utilized for the benefit of
those in whose name the *zins* are burned. This ceremony may be
celebrated every year on the occasion of a General Service; otherwise
every three, five, or seven years. In other parts of Haiti, for example in
the north and the northwest, it is completely unknown.

The ritual may vary from one Society to another in matters of detail
or in accordance with the loas served in the oum'phor. The *zins* are

small clay or cast iron cooking pots (the latter smaller than the former). Their true, secret name is *ouanzin*, and each rite has its own particular zin: the Rada zin is of pottery, as are also the Congo and the Ibo zins (on the "point" of Rada). The Nago zin, however, as also the Pethro, is of cast iron, is somewhat smaller than the Rada type, and usually has three small, high legs.

Ramise has been a mam'bo for many years. Her oum'phor, a rather important one, is located in the Cul-de-Sac Plain. At the beginning of the General Service which she celebrates every two years, she is accustomed to hold the *boulé-zins caille* in honor of all the loas of her oum'phor. For this occasion she invites several other Societies who come sometimes from great distances to be with her when she fulfills her obligations.

Sacrificing A Bull For The Simbi

The service about to be described took place in a large oum'phor located in Haite's Cul-de-Sac Plain. Numerous small, one or two room thatched huts—dwellings of the *pitit caille* or members of the Voodoo Society—are scattered about the vast area surrounding the oum'phor. Here, many ancient trees, chiefly mahogany and mango, furnish oases of coolness, a pleasant refuge from the burning heat of the harsh September sun. Most of the trees are reposoirs of Voodoo loas. Round about, fields of sugar cane nod in the breeze. The air is bracing—this is the open country.

The great peristyle is located in the middle of the yard facing the Rada inner oum'phor. The Péthro and Congo holy of holies are a little farther removed and off to one side, and in front of them stands another peristyle; somewhat smaller than the first, but equally ornate inside. Here the service for Simbi is about to be celebrated. Dieucifor, houn'gan and chief of the Society, is engaged in last-minute preparations, surrounded by a bevy of houn'sihs, all of them barefoot and dressed in white and wearing large foulards tied around their heads Mostly they are dark-skinned country women, sturdy and strong, with supple limbs and laughing eyes.

The dirt floor of the peristyle has been carefully swept and sprinkled. Dieucifor approaches the center-post, orients a jug of water, pours a few drops three times in front of the post, and then traces a very large vèvè on the ground completely encircling it. The tracing is made with several kinds of flour and assorted powders—cornmeal, ashes, coffee-grounds, brick dust, powdered bark and roots—while the vèvè itself comprises the various symbols of the mystères to whom the food is to be offered. The escorts of these loas are also to be invited.

Inasmuch as a bull will be sacrificed, a symbolic representation of a bull is included in the vèvè along with symbols of Simbi, Grand Bois, Maître Calfou, and several more loas. In the inner oum'phor, in front of the *pé*, a large hole is dug around which another and simpler vèvè is traced. Over the hole stands a table covered with a white cloth.

The table is spread with food and various kinds of desserts—cakes, candies, pastries, custards, chocolate, and rice pudding—as well as bottles of syrup, cola, liqueurs, rum, and clairin. All this is for the mystères who will appear. The cooked food will also be served on this table. When the table is cleared, all the food not consumed by the loas is placed in the hole. The choicest portions are, of course, saved, and most of it is given to the houn'gan's family and to the other members of the Society.

About ten o'clock in the morning the ogan clangs in the yard summoning the houn'sihs to the peristyle. They all hurry to enter, and seat themselves on benches and chairs around the central area. Two drummers are in their places, each holding a Péthro drum between his legs. The houn'sihs who form the chorus are grouped around them. The houn'guénicon comes out of the group and entones the opening chant, which is taken up by the chorus. The drums begin the Péthro beat:

Honneur la maison! (ter)	Greetings to the house! (3 times)
Honneur Maîtresse caille moin.	Greetings to the lady of my house.
M'crié: Honneur la maison!	I cry: Greetings to the house!
Messieurs et Dames, bonsoir.	Gentlemen and ladies, good evening.

A confiance unfastens the great ceremonial whip from the center-post, and, going outside, cracks it furiously in ritual fashion. The whip-cracking is punctuated by strident blasts of a whistle. A houn'sih comes out of the inner oum'phor with a jug of water and a lighted candle, followed by a few more carrying couis, glass tumblers, and bottles. A salutation is given and all the articles are set down beside the center-post. One of the painted couis contains the *manger djior* (a mixture of corn and roasted peanuts), and another holds a wide

assortment of bread, cassava, molasses-cakes, biscuits, and pastries. A
large glass is filled with *eau Guinin*, a mixture of food and water.
Other small containers hold custards, chocolate, coffee, and cane syrup.
Next to these are bottles of syrup, cola, liqueur, rum, clairin, and
finally a bottle of *kimanga* wrapped in green cloth trimmed in red.
The sacrificial animals have been carefully bathed in a solution of
leaves and lotion, then dried, and curried for a long time. At the moment of their entrance into the peristyle they are sprinkled with perfume. The young black bull is draped with a red and white mantle
decorated with red ribbons. A foulard of fiery satin is tied around the
horns. Two male goats, tan and yellow with black spots, wear coverings made of strips of cloth sewn together—each a different hue, for
each loa has its characteristic color, although the color of any given
loa may vary in accordance with the "point" upon which it is
"served." One of the coverings is yellow and rose, trimmed in blue;
the other is yellow, red, and green. One goat wears a white satin foulard on its horns, the other a foulard of red satin. The goats are held
on leashes, but the bull, somewhat too obstreperous, must be tied to
a firm post in the peristyle. The houn'sihs carry an imposing number
of roosters and hens with which they have been entrusted. The houn'-
guénicon starts the second introductory chant:

Legba man hounfor moin. (ter)	Legba, who is in my oum'phor.
Ou minm' qui pôté drapeau,	(3 times)
cé ou minm' qu'a paré soleil	You who carry the flag,
pou moin.	It is you who will protect me
Papa Legba man hounfor moin.	from the sun.
(ter)	Papa Legba, who is in my oum'-
Ou minm' qui pôté drapeau,	phor. (3 times)
cé ou minm' qu'a paré soleil	You who carry the flag,
pou loa yo.	It is you who will protect the loas
	from the sun.

Dieucifor comes in and consecrates the vèvè by shaking his asson
over its various parts while pronouncing the ritual formulas. The jug
of water is presented to him with the customary salutations. He orients it and pours out a few drops three times on all sides of the vèvè.
The chanting continues, greeting the Péthro and the Congo loas, while
the drums alter their rhythms to give the appropriate accompani-
ments. The houn'sihs, keeping their places, sway to the music. La

place comes out of the inner oum'phor leading two houn'sihs who
carry the spangled, embroidered and goldfringed flags that flap and
sparkle as they are rapidly waved from side to side. Approaching the
center-post, la place and the flag-bearers salute the four cardinal
points, then turn towards Dieucifor who faces them, holding the asson
and bell. The houn'gan and the flag-bearers salute the four "façades,"
after which Dieucifor makes la place and the houn'sihs *virer* (make
the ritual turns) and kiss the sword and the flags three times. The
visiting houn'gans and mam'bos are greeted by means of the same
ceremony.

The houn'gan seats himself on a low chair that someone has just
placed before the vèvè, and two mambos take their places on either
side of him. The prayer begins in the customary fashion, following the
Roman Catholic ritual. Then come the hymns, the litanies, and the
prière Dijor, which enumerates at great length the names of all the
loas. The houn'sihs, deep in meditation, and kneeling or squatting
around the vèvè, devoutly kiss the ground whenever the houn'gan
calls out the names of the mystère, particularly those who are especially honored in this oum'phor. The *prière Guinin* includes only the
Péthro and the Congo mystères, for the Rada mystères were greeted
during the course of previous services.

The prayers continue for more than an hour and a half. At the final
chant Dieucifor arises, takes the water-jug and the lighted candle, and
solemnly orients them to the four cardinal points. All the members of
the Society stand and go through the same gestures. The houn'gan
casts water on the four sides of the center-post, which he then kisses
three times.

For the consecration of the vèvè, Dieucifor takes successively the
various couis and other containers that are presented to him by a
houn'sih with the prescribed salutations. In deep meditation he orients
them, all the while pronouncing the invocations. He then kneels and
places on various parts of the vèvè little piles of the grain and the
different foods, to which he adds a bit of the contents of each bottle.

The chants resound once more in the peristyle:

Saluez moin Gangan, saluez
  moin.
A Apo Legba, saluez moin,
Gangan, saluez.
Papa m'cé pitit' Boucan Maza;

Salute me, Houn'gan, salute me.
A Apo Legba, salute me,
Houn'gan, salute.
My father is the child of Boucan
  Maza;

Papa m'cé pitit' Brisé Montagne.	My father is the child of Brisé
Oue, saluez moin, saluez moin o;	Montagne.
Papa m'cé pitit' Silamoyo.	Yes, salute me, oh salute me;
	My father is the child of Silamoyo.

Recitative:

Oui! Saluez moin, Brisé Mon-	Yes, Salute me, Brisé Montagne,
tagne,	Break-bones, Break-limbs,
Crazé-les-os, Crazé-les-membres,	Nèg' Kassa Bambila, Bila Congo,
Nèg' Kassa Bambila, Bila Congo,	Bila Louvemba;
Bila Louvemba;	Salute me, Houn'gan.
Saluez moin, Gangan.	

Little piles of gunpowder are finally placed upon the vèvè. A confiance brings a firebrand from the ritual fireplace out in the yard. Orienting the firebrand, Dieucifor makes the sign of the cross with it before the face of each houn'sih, then touches and ignites each pile of gunpowder with it. The glowing firebrand is extinguished with water while the whole assemblage cries out: *"Adjioh!"*

Caille moin, senti foulah,	My house feels the spray,
O Toutou Bilango.	Oh Toutou Bilango.
Macaya, m'senti foulah.	Macaya, I feel the spray.
Trois feuilles, Trois points,	Three leaves, Three points,
m'senti foulah!	I feel the spray!
Toutou Bilango.	Toutou Bilango.
Caille ô, O caille ô,	Oh house, Oh house, Oh,
caille moin senti foulah,	My house feels the spay,
Toutou Bilango!	Toutou Bilango!

A confiance brings the houn'gan the bottle of *kimanga*. In accordance with the Péthro ritual, the confiance holds it in his right hand and rapidly moves it at chest level to the left, to the right, and back again to the left. He then presents it directly to the houn'gan who quickly grasps it. However, it is not immediately released to him. Held by the two men, the bottle is moved upwards and from side to side until finally the confiance suddenly lets go of it; whereupon the houn'gan raises it over his head and everybody cries out: *"Adjioh!"* Still standing before the center-post, Dieucifor solemnly and slowly "vaporizes" the liquid contained in the bottle to the four cardinal points, blowing it across his bent forearm. More cries of *"Adjioh! Adjioh man!"* All the houn'sihs,

standing, turn in unison toward the four "façades" and curtsey gracefully. Dieucifor turns towards the drums and "vaporizes." He does the
same a moment later before the vèvè. Then, turning around, Dieucifor
"vaporizes" three times in succession across each arm bent at the elbow.
The "vaporized" *kimanga* is referred to as *kiman*.

The houn'sihs who hold the roosters and hens prepared for the sacrifice come forward. Dieucifor, summoning to his side two or three mam'-
bos, selects and distributes to each a rooster and a hen of matched
plumage. In a harmonious, combined movement they elevate and present the birds to the four cardinal points, at the same time pronouncing
the formula of orientation in subdued voices. This offertory gesture is
made very slowly, and the dignity of the ceremonial is enhanced by
the pure whiteness of the houn'sihs' dresses.

Dieucifor and the mam'bos, at first kneeling and holding the chickens
in their hands, rise and proceed to place them, one after the other, before the piles of food that adorn certain areas of the vèvè. As a rule,
the chickens do not hesitate to peck at it. Dieucifor kneels near the
center-post. Each mam'bo comes and carefully passes the hens over
him—from head to foot, back, face, and sides. Each completes this ritual
by striking him three times on the chest with the chicken. The ritual is
repeated over each person participating in the service. The houn'gan
begins a chant to summon the mystères. The names are called of all
the loas, particularly the Simbis, loas especially important in the Congo
and the Péthro rites. At each name the chorus responds in a subdued
voice; "*Batala oo Batala!*"

Houn'gan:	Chorus:
Batalua oo Batala, hé	Ian Pong'oué
Simbi Yandézo	Batala oo Batala
Simbi Congo	Batala oo Batala
Simbi Yan Paka	Batala oo Batala
Hé Ian Pong'oué!	Batala oo Batala
Simbi Yan Kita	

(Other names follow, each answered by the chorus.)

The pairs of roosters and chickens are crossed with water and with
flour. Some of the *manger djior* and a few drops of liqueur are put on
their backs. Dieucifor then "vaporizes" for the last time, and facing
the center-post and the inner oum'phor, slowly elevates the first
rooster holding it away at arm's length. With quick strokes he breaks

the wings and the feet as he pronounces the ritual formulas. Entering the Péthro inner temple he rips out the tongue and, using blood from the wound, sticks a few of the crop feathers upon various parts of the *pé*. Returning to the peristyle, he likewise sticks feathers upon the center-post and the vèvè. Meanwhile, one of the mambos has broken the wings and feet of the hen previously paired with the rooster by striking it against the center-post. All the houn'sihs fall on their knees as the two chickens are dispatched with a knife. The spurting blood from the cut throats is collected in a plate that is promptly placed at the base of the center-post. The singing resounds with even greater force. The bodies of the sacrificed chickens flap about on the blood-stained ground, and, quiet at last, are placed side by side with their heads upon the vèvès of the particular loas to whom they have been offered as sacrifices. Another rooster and chicken are now presented for the Marassa Péthro loas while the chanting continues:

Marassas Simbi,	Simbi Marassas,
m'engagé dans pays-a.	I am involved with this country.
Marassas Guinin, Marassas la Côté,	African Marassas, Coastal Marassas,
Marassas l'Afrique,	African Marassas,
n'engagé lan pays-a!	I am involved with this country.

The second pair of chickens, like the first pair, are placed upon the vèvè of the peristyle and encouraged to peck at the food offerings. Then they are removed to the vèvè in the inner oum'phor of Simbi where the whole performance is repeated. They are likewise passed over the body of the houn'gan and over all those present, consecrated, and finally sacrificed. This time, however, after the wings and legs have been broken and the tongue torn out, their necks are wrung. The remaining score of roosters and hens are simultaneously sacrificed.

All the houn'gans and mam'bos rise, holding the different colored chickens entrusted to them. These chickens are ritually oriented with all the dignity customarily observed on such occasions. The officiants move their lips in the sacred prayers. The four cardinal points are saluted, and the feet and wings of the birds are broken before the final sacrifice. Feathers fly in all directions over the vèvès as the chickens flap about, twitching and somersaulting until they expire.

In accordance with the ritual of the various loas in the train of

Simbi who are served nowadays, the throats of the chickens are usually cut with a knife rather than wrung. The first drops of bood are spilled on the vèvès, and the rest is collected in a dish. Each time the chickens are placed upon the vèvè of the mystère to whom the sacrifice is dedicated.

A woman about fifty years of age suddenly jumps backwards. The mystère Brisé has just "descended into her head." The possessed woman rises at once and proceeds over to the chickens just sacrificed. All the houn'sihs, on their knees now, wait to be raised to their feet by the mystère, whirled around, and given the Péthro salute. This type of greeting is given by gently striking the elbows three times while the arms are three-quarters bent. Brisé sways and gives the impression of dancing, uttering from time to time his customary cry: "*Guéguégué!*" He grinds his teeth and staggers as though drained of all energy.

When the goats are lead in, the cracking of whips and the sharp blasts of the whistle grow louder outside. The drum beat louder and the singing becomes more intense. The tawny, black-spotted goat is the first to be brought to the foot of the center-post. Its fine silk mantle is a rich adornment, and the red satin bows on its horns contrast vividly with the houn'sihs' white dresses. A large cross is traced on the goat's back, first with flour, next with water from the jug, and then with the "Guinea" water from the glass tumbler. Likewise a little of each pile of food and of each beverage is placed on its back, after which the containers (glasses or couis) are oriented. Next, a handful of *zerb Guinin* (Guinea grass) is handed to the houn'gan, which he receives and orients as he pronounces the ritual formula. He then goes to the goat, kneels before it, makes the sign of the cross, strikes each side of its head three times, grasps it by the horns, butts his own forehead three times against the goat's head, and rises. Every person in attendance comes up in hierarchic order and kneels before the goat, whose only interest during the proceedings is in chewing a few blades of the Guinea grass.

A little "Guinea water" is poured into a coui and presented to the goat. He drinks. Dieucifor takes the bottle of *kimanga* and sprays the goat "to the four façades." The leash and mantle are removed. Two strong assistants seize the goat, one by the horns, the other by the hind legs. They swing it back and forth three times, raise it off the ground three times, swing it again three times towards the four cardinal points, present it first before the entrance of the Péthro and the Congo inner oum'phor, and finally before the center-post. Some of the houn'sihs form a cortège behind the goat under the direction of la place and the flag-bearers. They circle the post several times in accordance with the ritual, first in one direction and then in the other, while the attendants continue to swing the goat from side to side. Singers and drummers go wild:

> Koumba cabrite télékou é.
> Koumba, koumba cabrite, télékiou é,
> cabrite télékou . . .

With a quick movement the goat is thrown on its back and a cross is traced on its body with a sharp knife held by a confiance. Its testicles are quickly severed and squeezed lightly until a few drops of blood trickle out upon the vèvè and in the interior of the bagui. Still held with its feet in the air, the goat is slain with knife thrust in its neck (the knife having previously been oriented). Blood gushes forth into a large wooden basin reserved for this purpose, into which salt and alcohol had already been placed. The goat is held in the air until only a slight trickle of blood remains. It is then laid on the ground.

The other goat is consecrated and sacrificed in exactly the same way as the first, the ceremony being repeated right up through the final sacrifice. Then a new chant begins:

Toute famille a yo semblé.	The whole family is assembled.
La famille semblé.	The family as assembled.
Hé, créoles, ô nous là.	Hey, Créoles, Oh, here we are.
Ago yé!	Ago yé!
La famille semblé.	The family is assembled.
Nan point Guinin encô.	Africa no longer exists.

The bodies of the goats, together with the severed testicles, are placed upon the vèvè. The sign of the cross is made over them as well as over the heap of dead chickens. A white plate upon which a cross has been graced with flour is placed over them. This is for the "adoration" ceremony to which all those present are now invited in the words of the following song:

Vin payer sang;	Come and pay for the blood;
cérémonie-a belle ô.	the ceremony is beautiful.

La famille vin prayer sang, non!	The family comes to pay for the blood.
Cérémonie-a belle ô.	The ceremony is beautiful.
O Aayo,	Oh Aayo,
la famille vin prayer sang!	the family comes to pay for the blood!

Dieucifer comes and kneels before the vèvè holding money in each hand. He speaks at great length with the mystères before placing the money in the plate, first with the right hand, then with the left, as with firm conviction he makes his "demand."

The bodies of all the sacrificed animals are picked up and removed by the houn'sihs who are to prepare them according to ritual practice. The soiled ground is swept, and all the sweepings are carefully collected in a coui and taken away.

The sacrifice of the bull is next. The bull is tied to a post in the peristyle a little to one side. The central area is enlarged by making the people move back their chairs, thus leaving more space around the bull. Dieucifor prepares to consecrate the animal according to ritual, but it is not easy to keep it in check. Only with difficulty does he hold in place the mantle, which has a tendency to slip off on one side because nobody dares get close enough to adjust it. The houn'-gan presents the bull with the coui containing the "Guinea water." When the bull has tasted it, the houngan offers a handful of "Guinea grass." Placing himself in front of the bull he speaks to it at some length, then holds out some stalks to it. Chant succeeds chant without a break, while the houn'sihs dance in their places or simply sway back and forth.

Simbi lan barrière;	Simbi is at the gate;
z'aut' poco connin moin.	the others do not yet know me.
Ala nous rivé	Well, we have arrived;
nous pr'allé gâté coumandé.	we are going to disregard the order,
Yé! Simbi Yandézo,	Yeh! Simbi Yandézo,
Ian Paka Pong'oué!	Ian Paka Pong'oué!
M'di: Yé! Kim'boi salay!	I say: Yeh! Kim'boi salay!
Salam a salay!	Salam a salay!
Simbi lan barrière;	Simbi is at the gate;
z'aut' poco connin moin.	the others do not yet know me.

The bull is consecrated. Dieucifor stands beside the animal and draws crosses down the entire length of its back with water from the jug, with flour, and with the *manger djior* and other food offerings. The nervous animal rears up unexpectedly from time to time as he feels the syrup or the cola trickling over his head and flanks. The chants grow louder and louder:

Zo, Aidé Zo,	Zo, Aidé Zo,
tabatiè'm tombé;	my snuff-box falls down;
côté m'a joinn' li?	where shall I find it?
Zo, Aidé Zo. (ter)	Zo, Aidé Zo. (three times)
Oui! O Kim'boi ma salay!	Yes, Oh Kim'boi ma salay!
Simbi Yan Paka! Simbi Ian Dézo!	Simbi Yan Paka! Simbi Ian Dézo!
Oui! Simbi Ian Kita!	Yes, Simbi Ian Kita!
Grande Adjiakonver, Grande Simba!	Grande Adjiakonver, Grande Simba!

Suddenly a woman is mounted by a bull-mystère who moos loudly. This mystère is Bélécou, but so overwhelming is he that he cannot remain very long. A Simbi loa, Ian Paka Pong'oué, possesses a wizened, gnarl-jointed man about sixty years old. The possession at first is violent. Simbi arrives and departs, his gestures stiff, angular, and bizarre. However, his grim expression softens whenever he greets someone he is fond of: the scowl on his face vanishes, the contractions of his jaws gradually cease. He gives the Péthro salute by striking his elbows against the elbows of the other person, then hooks his little finger in the little finger of the other person to make him *virer* (turn around upon himself).

The houn'gan sprays the *kiman* over the arms of Simbi, and very tightly fastens on him a blood-red foulard. Flaming clairin is poured on the ground in front of the mystère, who then stamps on it with great force. The mystère then takes his leave.

While the houn'gan and mam'bos were consecrating the bull, the houn'sihs were greeting Simbi with several songs, among them:

Papa Simbi Racine Coumandé,	Papa Simbi Racine Coumandé,
Feuilles-non-bois,	Leaves-in-the-woods,
cé moin-minme, Racine o o o o!	it is I, Racine, Oh, Oh, Oh, Oh!
Simbi Ian Dézo, Racine Coumandé!	Simbi Ian Dézo, Racine Coumandé!

Feuilles-nan-bois,	Leaves-in-the-woods,
cé nou-minme, Racine o o o o!	it is we, Racine, Oh, Oh, Oh, Oh!

Dieucifor summons his nephew, a young man about twenty years old, who he also allows to consecrate the bull despite the fact the latter is not a houn'gan. All at once the young man is mounted by a Simbi, the particular Simbi whom his family "serves." He looks utterly different; his perfectly ordinary peasant features become those of a young, fiery god, vigorous, yet somewhat fawn-like. With amazing agility he leaps upon the bull's back, remains there a moment, and then sinks back to the ground. He immediately tries again, and by leaning lightly with one hand on the animal, clears the obstacle. The bull rears, excited, and paws the ground with his hoof. A woman possessed by another Simbi leaps up in turn on the bull's neck and grasps its horns. The first Simbi jumps behind the second, and now both of them together straddle the menacing, foaming animal as he lowers his head and butts against the post with dull thuds, releasing all his pent-up violence. Deafening cries of "Adjioh" and Bilolo" resound in the peristyle. In this way Simbi demonstrates his satisfaction with the offerings. However, Dieucifor is worried. He would like to temper somewhat the exuberant enthusiasm of the mystères, for he is afraid to let them revel at will. Should they happen to untie the bull and lead it around the neighborhood, he might have a lot of trouble with the local authorities. So he prefers to use persuasion to get the Simbis to dismount before he orders them to depart.

The bull is untied and with powerful strides moves out of the peristyle, preceded by the flag-bearers under the direction of the sword-brandishing la place. Everyone is on his feet now. Confusion reigns as all join the procession moving behind the bull toward the gate where Simbi and Grand Chemin are to be greeted. Excitement increases. Flags wave and flap, embroidered pennants sparkling in the bright sun. La place makes the flag-bearers double step, reverse their pace, and circle around the tree-reposoirs in a whirl of satin flags. Quick flashes of light dart from his sword blade. The white-robed houn'sihs encircle the bull, exciting him with their songs and cries of "Adjioh" and "Bilolo!"

After the salutation at the gate, the cortège returns on the double to the peristyle. From all over the neighborhood members of the cult leave their thatched houses to join the crowd. Three times they go around the peristyle on the outside, and then proceeding inside make a turn about the center-post. The heavy tramping of the bull can be heard. The general excitement has reached its peak. Children join the adults to dance and squeal with delight. "Bilolo!" A passage is cleared. Everyone rushes in so as not to miss the spectacle.

The bull is lead to one end of the yard to the ritual spot where the bulls are always sacrificed. All of the audience who had joined in the mad procession, singing and dancing, form a large circle and intone a chant appropriate to the occasion, to the hammering, clanking accompaniment of the ogan:

Moin nan sang korali ouan-nié,	I am in the blood of korali ouan-nié,
En yé!	Eh yeh!
Moin nan sang	I am in the blood of
Simbi lan Dézo, Simbi Ian Paka.	Simbi lan Dézo, Simbi Ian Paka.
Allez mander Jean-Pierre Pong'-oué.	Go and ask Jean-Pierre Pong'oué.
Ya yé, moin nan sang hé!	Yah, yeh, I am in the blood, hey!

The houn'sihs clap their hands in time, swaying to the music, while the official sacrificer slowly orients the knife, traces, a cross upon the bull, makes three feigned strokes, and finally, with a single thrust plunges in the blade just behind the neck. Almost at once the bull falls to his knees and dies in the midst of howling and screaming.

Mam'bo Miracia Treats The Sick

A sick man whose illness is considered very grave has just been brought to the oum'phor. He is a peasant from the great Cul de Sac Plain, a man in fairly comfortable circumstances, who frequently visits Port-au-Prince to take care of his affairs. He is a well-built fellow about thirty years old, apparently struck down in full health by a malady as sudden as it is violent. From the onset of the attack his family was worried, as his symptoms lead them to fear some supernatural intervention.

Consequently, one of the man's relatives hastened to pay a "visit" to the neighborhood houn'gan who, after laying out a few playing cards in a *layé*, a flat bamboo bark basket, revealed that certain dead spirits had been "sent" after the poor fellow and that he had been "given" to Baron Samedi, Lord of the Cemetery. Counter measures are most urgently required to forestall his death.

The members of his family got together and decided to ask Miracia, the mam'bo of La Saline, if she would agree to "treat" the sick man. When Miracia understood what they wanted, she immediately referred the matter to her personal mystères—in particular to Brisé, the great "Work Chief" of her oum'phor who, when consulted, promised to undertake the treatment.

After shaking her cockle-shells over the *layé*, Miracia informed the family that not merely one, but three dead spirits had been "sent." She also disclosed several other pertinent items of information. Accordingly, as soon as they had reached an understanding with the mam'bo about the projected treatment, the sick man was brought to the oum'phor; for if no treatment whatever had been attempted, he would surely have died.

That night he was laid out in the peristyle on a mat next to the center-post. He appeared extremely ill and was very nearly unconscious. He neither spoke nor moved, seemed abnormally weak, and had not eaten for fifteen days. The family brought all the items necessary for the ceremony to be performed in accordance with the mam'bo's instructions.

In the *Caille-Guédé*, the inner chamber of the oum'phor dedicated to the loa Guédé, a vèvè representing a coffin with handles on the sides was traced on the floor with ashes and coffee-grounds. The patient's measurements had previously been taken by means of a small knotted cord. Two small, old mats were oriented and placed upon the vèvè, completely covering it. Then the sign of the cross was made over the mats with ashes.

On a table three small *couis* were prepared containing a mixture of corn grains and roasted peanuts, and in the middle of each a small candle was set, on white, one yellow, and one black. Next to the *couis* was placed a bottle of clairin and a bottle of *kimanga*—a potent alcoholic ritual beverage, usually employed in the Pethro rite and varying in composition according to the tastes of the loas for whom it is prepared. Under the table was placed a large *coui* and two *gamelles* containing a darkish bath liquid consisting of ox-gall and other ingredients.

At length, Maracia orders the patient to be brought in. First, however, his attendants are obliged to remove their clothes and put them on again inside out—an absolutely necessary precaution.

Nevertheless, the dead spirits are apparently getting suspicious that steps are being taken to drive them away, for the moment the attendants try to bring in the patient, one of the spirits speaking through his mouth declares that, do what they will, he will not depart; they will not succeed in driving him away; instead, he will grow even stronger. Those standing within earshot reply to the effect that "We'll see who's the stronger!"

Only with difficulty can they lift the sick man, even by supporting him below the arms. They nearly have to carry him on account of his extreme weakness. Now and then the voice of one of the spirits can be heard muttering defiance to the mam'bo. Clad in a long white nightshirt, the patient at length falteringly enters the *Caille-Guédé* and is made to recline on the mats covering the vèvè. His head rests upon a large stone just at the foot of a large cross of black wood. His nightshirt is removed and he wears only a pair of white shorts. Not a word comes from his lips. His eyes are closed, or only half open, and totally without expression.

A white cloth is rolled into a *bande-mâchoire* or chin-band, placed under his jaws and tied on top of his head as though he were a corpse. Another band, narrower, binds his two big toes together. His arms are stretched alongside his body, palms up.

His entire body is "crossed" with ashes. The small *couis* containing the burning candles are placed one at each shoulder and one at the feet. In another *coui* filled with *roroli* (sesame seeds) burns a bit of incense and asafoetida. The brownish stone belonging to Brisé is placed in its white plate near the patient's head.

The small chamber serving as the *Caille-Guédé* will scarcely hold a dozen people, inasmuch as the patient, stretched out in the center of the floor, occupies most of the space. An ancient lantern hangs on the wall, while a large taper set upon the masonry *pé* forming the base of the cross furnishes a dim, smokey light. Various wierd objects on the *pé* can be seen in the shadows; other furniture forms a dark, indistinguishable mass. Stones rubbed with oil reflect a dim gleam from the plate on which they repose. Occasionally a row of bottles sparkles in a ray of light. Here and there several *couis* can be distinguished, decorated with the various attributes of the Barons and the Guédés—the skull and crossbones, the shovels, the picks and axes of the gravedigger painted white upon black with a few touches of gray or purple. On the wall hang the old clothes worn by the Guédés when they "mount" their "horses." A grotesque battered stovepipe hat perches crazily on a table next to a cigar.

A short Roman Catholic prayer is spoken by the mam'bo, followed by several others "offered" especially for the task at hand, as for example the prayer of St. Expeditus. Miracia always begins with the same words: "In the name of God the Father, God the Son, and God the Holy Ghost, in the name of Mary, in the name of Jesus, in the name of all the saints, all the dead . . . " She concludes by asking all the mystères to lend their presence this evening "with God's permission," in order that He may grant success to her undertaking. When all the djohouns, or Voodoo mystères of Guinée (Africa) have been thus called, a special invocation is pronounced in langage, addressed to certain of these mystères more directly associated with the present task.

At the conclusion of the prayers, small piles of corn and roasted peanuts, as well as the manger djior,—a ritual preparation consisting of bread, cassava, plantain, and the peelings of green plantains—are placed upon the abdomen, the chest, the forehead, and in the palm of each of the patient's hands. Miracia takes a chicken—a hen—of dark, variegated plumage, together with a yellowish-white coq frisé. The two birds are oriented in turn, and then the hen is held in front of each small pile and encouraged to peck at it, moving from the pile on the right hand to that on the left, then to the abdomen, the chest, and the forehead. The same thing is done with the cock, while Miracia pronounces sotto voce the prescribed invocations. A huge red rooster—a splendid bird with marvellous spurs, such as is used only for this type of treatment—is brought in, oriented, and likewise placed before the little piles and induced to peck at them. However, he does this with such violence that the sick man starts up in fear when the bird reaches his forehead. Miracia reassures him of the beneficial treatment the sick always receive at her place: "My treatment won't make a 'martyr' of anybody." Nevertheless, just to play it safe, someone holds his hand over the patient's eyes. The red rooster is then placed between the man's legs, the head in his crotch, while the chicken and the coq frisé are set side by side upon his chest, one on the right side, the other on the left, with their heads stretched out towards his middle.

More invocations and prayers both in *langage* and in Créole are spoken. Then the mam'bo gets up and takes the chicken in one hand and the *coq frisé* in the other. She orients them, pronouncing the sacred words, and "passes" them somewhat brusquely over the sick man, almost touching him. During the entire operation she pronounces the prescribed words: *Tout ça qui mauvais cé pour sorti, tout ça qui bon cé pour entré* (All that is evil, depart; all that is good, enter). As a leit-motiv, the refrain repeats: *Enté, té, té, tété, té . . .*

The mam'bo has a curious habit of crossing and uncrossing the man's arms, all the while holding the chickens just above his body, but only touching or slightly grazing his skin. These movements are principally made over the chest, then over the entire torso, and finally down the length of the arms. From time to time the man starts up violently, but he is ordered to relax quietly and to keep his head on the stone. This order, however, is really addressed to the dead spirits who have taken their abode in his body as much as to the patient.

Tirelessly Miracia requests the mystères to "release" the sick man and to "give him back his life," "with God's permission." The name of Brisé is cited in particular, as well as that of Aguroi-Linsou, who belongs to the Guédé group of mystères and who loves to "dance" in the mam'bo's head. Others invoked are Guédé Nouvavou, Guédé Houn-Sou, and Guédé Mazaca. Interspersed among the names of these mystères appear the names of various deceased members of the patient's family, called the "Danti" or chieftains of his race. The hen and the cock, separately and together, are then carefully passed over his entire body. After each passage the birds are held to one side away from the body and shaken, as though to remove whatever evil influence they may have absorbed from it.

The chickens are then placed upon the ground, and Miracia asks someone to hand her the *coq frisé*, which she turns loose in the yard. People believe that this bird at a given moment mysteriously disappears, possibly within a few days. It is the first hen passed over the. sick man, however, which extracts the exorcised spirits. The *coq-frisé*, on the other hand, removes the "lingering evil air."

Next, the three *couis*, in which the small candles have been burning since the beginning of the ceremony, are taken and passed one after the other over the patient from head to foot. They are moved over his forehead in a circle, and after they are placed on the ground again, the stone belonging to Brisé is solemnly oriented and passed over the

patient in the same manner. All the while Miracia continues the invocations with the recurring *Enté, té, té, té, té* . . . The invocation to
Brisé spoken by the mam'bo is "by the power of Brisé of the Mountain,
Break-bones, Break-limbs, *Neg cassa manbila bila congo, bila lou-
vimba.* After these orders for Pethro, Man of the Tozin pool, Man at
the Miragoâne Bridge."

The mam'bo then goes to the basin containing the "bath liquid,"
takes as much of it as she can hold in her cupped hands, and with a
quick, rough movement, fairly slaps it right at the sick man's head and
face. This performance is repeated several times, the man starting up
suddenly at the unexpected shower. He struggles, tries to raise his
head, and growls dismally. An attendant forces him to lie still but the
mam'bo remarks *Cé pas faute li; cé pas li minm qu'ap fait çà; cé
mort-à!* (It's not his fault; he isn't the one who's doing that; it's the
dead spirit.)

To keep this performance going several people in relays continue
to thrash the sick man with water—his face, head, neck, and torso.
They help him rise to a half-sitting position, the more easily to lash
him with packets of leaves, bark, and roots soaked in a brownish
liquid. Meanwhile, the chinband falls off in the struggle. The cord that
bound his two big toes together is loosed, and he is made to stand up.
His whole body drips water. The fellow in charge of this part of the
treatment is drenched in perspiration. The dead spirits trouble the
man's body, making him start up suddenly; they grumble and howl as
though beaten. The mam'bo keeps right on ordering them to depart,
threatening to employ any and all means to drive them out. A piece
of garlic is put in the patient's mouth. Soon a kind of quiet seems to
descend upon him, yet he appears curiously distant. He falls back on
the mat unconscious—the dead spirits have abandoned him.

Immediately the mambo leans over his recumbent figure and calls
out his name over and over again with great energy: *Ovril! Orvil!
Orvil! Cé ou? Cé ou qui là?* (Orvil! Orvil! Orvil! Is it you? Are you
there?) Fnally a feeble moan and a scarcely perceptible "yes" can
be heard. Instantly a confiance takes the bottle of clairin and pours
it over the stone of Brisé which lies in a plate, setting it on fire. He
takes this burning alcohol and passes it rapidly over the man's entire
body. He is held up gently so that this medication can be more easily
applied. Tiny bluish flames play over the confiance's hands but
quickly flicker out as they come in contact with the patient's damp

body. The mambo seizes the bottle of *kimanga* and sprays it out through her teeth several times over his body. After being vigorously massaged for a while, the patient appears to have regained a little strength. Most important of all: the expression on his face is completely different. His eyes have a weary look, but at any rate there is a human expression in them.

Miracia gives the signal to leave the *Caille-Guédé* and proceed several paces to the oum'phor yard where a large hole has been dug right next to the *reposoirs*. The trunk of a small, recently uprooted banana tree leans propped against another tree. It is about as tall as a man, and will be used to "redeem the patient's life."

The hole is encircled by a crown of seven small lamps made of oranges cut in half, scooped out, filled with castor oil, and furnished with a hand-twisted cotton wick. The three small *couis* are also brought out and arranged in the form of a triangle. The patient comes forth supported by the others, but appearing a little stronger than before. He is lowered into the hole in a standing position, facing towards the west, and holding the banana tree in his hands with the roots touching the ground at the bottom of the hole. The hen used earlier in the treatment is again passed over his entire body, while the mambo continues to utter the following invocations: "With the permission of God, the Saints, the Dead, by the power of Papa Brisé, Mr. Aguroi-Linsou, Mr. Guédé Nibo, Mr. Guédé Nouvavou, and All Guédés, I demand that you return the life of this man. I, mam'bo Yabofai, demand the life of this man. I buy for cash; I pay you; I owe you nothing!" The formulas in *langage* follow this invocation.

Next, Miracia takes the small *couis* one after the other, pours the contents in her hand, and rubs them over the man's body. They fall in the hole and remain there, and the *couis* are placed on the edge. She now takes a jug and quickly pours its contents over the man's head, and, holding it by the neck, lowers it behind the man down as far as the hole, breaks it with a solid blow, and lets the pieces fall into the hole.

Miracia then takes the hot oil from one of the small lamps in the hollow of her hand and rubs it on the patient. This action is repeated with oil from each of four lamps, and during this part of the ceremony somebody out in the yard keeps cracking a whip.

The mam'bo takes the chicken, holds it tightly together by bending its head against its body, and places it in the hole down against the roots of the banana tree. Squatting down, all at once she shoves a great quantity of dirt into the hole, while the *confiance*, supporting the patient under the arms, lifts him out and sets him down again beside the hole. This act is accomplished very quickly, and without losing any time the hole is filled up and the earth stamped down around the tree. The chicken is thus buried alive. Miracia never ceases to utter the necessary formulas designed to insure the success of the operation. The three remaining lamps are placed in the form of a triangle around the tree.

Clairin is poured as it was previously in the *Caille-Guédé* in the plate containing the stone of Brisé. The stone is ignited and passed over the patient who is now standing several feet away from the hole. Three small piles of gunpowder are placed on the ground in the form of a triangle where the man is standing with feet spread apart. After the gunpowder is ignited, Miracia again "sprays" some *kimanga* over and around him to the four cardinal points.

An undershirt, white with red patches, called a *maldjoc*, meaning "evil eye" or "bad luck," is produced, and a corner of it is twisted and slightly burned. Holding this roughened and scorched cloth in her hand Miracia traces several signs in the air before the face and body of the patient. She gives him the *maldjoc* to slip on. The long nightgown is handed to him before he is brought to the peristyle. He no longer needs to be supported, his walk is much steadier, and his eyes are brighter. A definite change has taken place in him.

In the peristyle a white handkerchief is knotted around his head in such a way as to cover it completely. His feet are washed, and he is given a very hot infusion of leaves to drink which had previously been prepared. Then he is told to lie down and keep well covered. The stone of Brisé is placed under his pillow.

The next morning the patient felt much better. He was able to get up by himself and wash. He spoke, and asked for something to eat for the first time since his fifteen days' fast. He was given some tea and vegetable broth. For dinner he requested some potato pancakes and a red herring. A veritable resurrection!

A patient under treatment should not, as a security measure, leave the oum'phor enclosure for any reason whatsoever, for he is not yet out of danger. The first hen that was passed over his body during the treatment in the *Caille-Guédé* removed the *expéditions* (the three dead spirits). The *coq frisé*, which was passed over him next, took

away the *reste mauvais air* (remaining evil air). The chicken which
was buried alive at the foot of the banana tree, together with the tree
itself, is supposed to have *racheter* (redeemed) the man's life. Baron
Samedi, chief loa of the cemetery, had been asked to graciously accept
this exchange of lives. But it was the Power, given through her Knowledge *(connaissance)*, that enabled the mam'bo to induce this mystère
to accept the barter.

If the man is to survive, the tree dies. If the tree lives, the man will
probably die, the bargain having been refused. The vèvè which was
traced on the floor of the *Caille-Guédé* cannot be swept away until the
man departs, cured or dead.

Ceremony of the Bark of Agoueh

A small boat is prepared, loaded with all kinds of food and drink
offerings preferred by the mystère Agoueh. A watch is maintained all
through the night in the oum'phor by houn'sihs, mambos, houn'gans,
and houn'tor-guis. The following day at early dawn it is loaded onto a
truck which transports it, together with the oum'phor personnel and
with drums, a trumpet, ritual flags, assons, the ritual flour for the
vèvès, the ritual machete of la place, candles, and other articles, to a
beach or to some spot near the shore. There the boat is carefully
loaded with everything that is going to be offered in sacrifice to the
mystère. A ceremony is held rapidly, after which a series of vèvès is
traced making a ring around the boat. The trumpet sounds, accompanied by drums and seashells used as horns. The flags, carried by
the houn'sihs *cò-drapeaux* (flag-bearers) and lead by la place armed
with his machete, salute both the ship and its cargo after being oriented to the four cardinal points. A houn'gan carries the loaded boat
upon his head down to another boat on the shore in which everybody
embarks. The boat hoists anchor to the sound of drums, ritual chants,
trumpet, and seashells, and heads out to sea.

Meanwhile a houn'gan lights an oil lamp made in a white cup, the
favorite color of Agoueh, which he places in the center of the bark at
the time of embarkation. The customary prayers are recited. The most
important member of the ceremony is without doubt the one upon
whom most of the attention has been paid since leaving the oum'phor,
namely a snow-white sheep. The sheep is also placed on board the

boat, and while the prayers are recited preparations are made to offer this sheep to the mystère of the sea, Maître Agoueh R O-yo, by casting it into the sea along with the bark, a pair of white pigeons, and a pair of white chickens, which the houn'sihs have constantly been waving in the air all during the sailing. The ritual bark is traditionally sent off to Ifé. It is there that the sheep and bark, pigeons and chickens are thrown into the sea at the moment when the drums and the houn'sihs go into a state of hallucinations and mystic frenzy. Then the bark returns from Ifé. During all the passage, the mam'bo who offers the sacrifice remains standing and leaning on the single mast facing the prow of the boat and agitating symbolically and magically the ritual oar of the Voodoo mystère. At no moment do the drums cease to beat. Upon returning, the ceremony is completed on the shore.

A Calendar of Voodoo Ceremonies

The following calendar of ceremonies primarily concerns the Voodoo seen in Port-au-Prince and its environs, because all the regions of Haiti do not practice Voodoo in the same manner when it comes to considering the differences in ritual of a single region. Just so, Voodoo is fundamentally the same everywhere, differences being due to the African groups that practice it. To all intents and purposes, these differences make it almost impossible to devise a Voodoo calendar with complete accuracy. For where a particular oum'phor in Arcahaié will hold a service traditionally set, for example, on June 15th, for the mystère Grande Aloumandia, the same mystère might be "served" at Léogane on May 2nd. The following table is therefore compiled from the elements of several oum'phors in order to give a general idea of Voodoo feasts:

January

2, 3, 4	Casé gâteaux (Breaking the cakes), a communal form of *manger-loa*
6	Les Rois (The Kings)

February

25   Manger têtes d'l'eau (Ritual feeding of springs)

March

16   Loko Davi (Eating of the ritual wood and of its guard)
19   Saint Joseph (Expression of the jurisdiction of Legba)
20   Legba Zaou (Eating consists mainly of a black goat and
      of *bananes laudanne*)

April

27   Dan Wédo, Clermeille
29   Cassé canarie (Breaking the jugs: deliverance of the souls
      from purgatory)
31   Mangé-les-morts (Feeding the dead: The *managers crus*
      are offered to the jugs or jars in which the souls are
      supposed to reside and where they eat; subsequently
      the *manger cuits* are offered them, particularly *gombo*
      or okra, *moussah*, Carib-cabbage)

May

12   Feeding of different loas
18   Feeding of Grande Aloumandia
20, 21   Sim'bi blanc
30   Chanté-messes (Sung masses in the Roman Catholic
          Churches), Martinique dances, Bamboches

June

24   Saint John
28   M'sieu Guimeh Sauveur; Mystère Gé Agoum' Tonnerre;
        Table served for Maîtresse Erzulie, Maîtresse Ténaise,
        Maîtresse Mam'bo (common table)

July

25   Papa Ogou (alias Saint James the Greater), to whom is
        offered particularly sheep and goats
26   Grande Saint Anne (alias Mystère Grande Délai and
        Grande Aloumandia; common table)
29   Maîtresse Silvérine, who only very slightly tastes of the
        food offered to her
        Maîtresse Lorvana, who smells flowers for her nourish-
        ment

August

25   Communion table for Dan Wédo (alias Saint Louis, King
        of France)
29   O-Dan; L'Orient, one of the most important mystères.
30, 31 Aga-ou (Offerings: particularly goats, peppers, pepper-
        mint)

September

25   Roi Wangol; Mousondi
29   Manman Aloumandia
30   Maîtresse Délai (A very important mystère who "walks"
        with the houn'tor: the voodoo tambourine player)

October

30, 31 Singing masses in the Roman Catholic Churches
Communion table
Martinique Dance
Armchair ritually covered with 30 or 40 scarves of different colors, exposed in the peristyle and "served"

November

1, 2 Bamboches for the Guédé mystères: the dead who come out of the cemeteries, possess their "horses," and come into the oum'phors to amuse themselves in the form of souls incarnated or reincarnated
25 Manger-yam (Eating the yams)

December

10 Ganga-Bois
12, 13, 14 Agoueh R Oyo (Feeding the sea)
25 Bath of Christmas
Leaf-rubbing (for medical treatments and talismans for magic protection)
Ritual sacrifices of pigs and goats
Bonfires (boucans) for amusement, to which the loas come to bathe themselves and their protégés
Sacrifice of turkeys for Caplaou